Choice and Challenge
for the American Woman

Choice and Challenge
for the
American Woman

Gladys Evans Harbeson

SCHENKMAN PUBLISHING COMPANY, INC.
CAMBRIDGE, MASSACHUSETTS

Two roads diverged in a wood, and I —
I took the one less traveled by,
And that has made all the difference.

ROBERT FROST

Table of Contents

world wars. Growth of the democratic ideal. Re-evaluation of women's aptitudes with the advent of experimental psychology. Erasing of psychological barriers to paid employment through modification of distinctions between classes.

patterns in Britain, Sweden, Africa, India, and Russia.
Unique challenge for the American woman.

List of Charts and Tables

Acknowledgments

The initial stimulus for preparing this study was provided some time ago by the publications of the Commission on the Education of Women of the American Council on Education. A subsequent review and evaluation of both popular and scholarly literature on the subject of the changing life patterns of modern women convinced me of the need to make available to a wider range of readers certain pertinent facts regarding these trends, as well as suggestions for formulating a theory of values which could assist the individual in her adaptation to the new patterns.

Of course, I cannot name here all of the many sources from which the facts presented in this book have been obtained. Publications of the Women's Bureau of the U.S. Department of Labor have been an especially rich source. I am particularly indebted to all publishers who have granted me permission to use materials which provide a glimpse of women's changing life patterns in international perspective.

I wish to thank the editors of the Schenkman Publishing Company for their suggestions, which have broadened the scope of this book. I am also grateful to the staff of the University of Illinois Library for providing special accommodations to facilitate my writing and research, and especially to my husband for his many helpful suggestions, and his encouragement in the writing of this book.

G. E. H.

Introduction

For women, life planning is something new. Men have long understood the necessity of a far-sighted program for their lives. As boys they dream of becoming physicians, architects, or engineers, and as young men they prepare for the occupations in which they expect to engage for a lifetime. But not until recent decades have women felt much need for a far look into their futures. Throughout the centuries their expectations, with few exceptions, have been only for marriage and enough education to make them acceptable as wives and homemakers. Nor was this complacency disturbed to any appreciable extent until the early years of the twentieth century when the possible alternative of marriage or career introduced a new dimension into their lives.

Today, young educated middle-class women are beginning to plan ahead for a long lifetime. The ever-widening variety of occupations now opening for them makes more comprehensive planning a requirement for satisfying living. Leading educators are telling us that we who perform a feminine role need not be confined to *choosing* among our multiple chances for love, marriage, and work, but that we can combine *all* of these experiences in larger self-fulfillment than that known to our mothers and grandmothers. This concept of living also implies a husband who will be a sympathetic partner.

What has brought about this change? The greatly lengthened life span, abundant educational opportunities, need for trained workers, labor-saving devices within the home and in industry, early community orientation of children — all of these factors, as well as a new social ideology, are influencing women to plan farther ahead what they will do with their lives.

Because feminine life patterns have much less continuity than those of men, involving sharp contrasts among various periods in the individual's life experience, we have a special need for developing perspective, a fact too often obscured for young women by the prospect of early marriage. But how can we obtain a perspective which will serve us functionally? First, we must acquire knowledge of the most promising present and future outlets for the use of women's talents and abilities, then prepare adequately for the use of our own, building for ourselves a storehouse from which to draw in times of later need. As Professor Mabel Newcomer, who has given many years of service to the women of Vassar College, points out:

> If we are not to drift, deal with the future we must. And while the risks of forecasting are many, it is not just a guessing game. If we can make up our minds what we want the future to be, we can in some measure shape it to that end.*

We can plan our futures intelligently only by first understanding how to fit our own individual life patterns into the larger social design. Why are mothers working outside their homes today more than did their mothers and grandmothers? How can mothers decide whether or not to enter gainful employment? If they do, at what time in their lives? With increasing employment of women, how can values be maintained in the home? What effect does a mother's employment have upon her children? In what ways are the scope and purpose of homemaking enlarged today? Why is education more important for women now than even a decade ago? What sort of college education is best for daughters? How can young women prepare themselves both for the major task of homemaking and for outside employment at some time in their lives? What occupations offer the greatest demand for women's services? What is meant by the newly emphasized concept of feminine self-fulfillment?

The first chapters of this book are designed to help us perceive that the personal desire for a larger measure of self-fulfillment which many of us come to feel especially in our middle and later years is universally felt by truly educated women. Later chapters survey the potential of women in modern American society. They give a glimpse of new designs in education intended to prepare us for assuming the dual role of homemaker and paid employee. They suggest methods of keeping our professional and cultural interests alive during the child-rearing period, and opportunities now developing for us to continue

* Mabel Newcomer, *A Century of Higher Education for American Women* (New York: Harper & Brothers Publishers, 1959), p. 245.

professional education when our responsibilities for rearing our families begin to slacken.

But considering each of these matters separately does not uncover the root of an underlying problem. Must our years of formal education, followed by those of homemaking, then our later return to a professional pursuit be characterized by contradictory orientations? The basic fact is that we need to discover a fundamental purpose which will fuse the several parts of our lives into a harmonious whole. If we as American women can unify our purpose so as to preserve constant basic values throughout the several segments of our life experience, we will have fulfilled an obligation not only to ourselves, but to our nation and to women of other cultures who share our problems and stand in need of imaginative leadership. Only by our achieving such harmony within our lives can we fully realize today's bright promise of richer self-fulfillment for women.

CHAPTER 1

The Evolution of the Feminine Role

What has not been seen is the more general point that for the first time, in the history of any known society, motherhood has become a full-time occupation for adult women.

ALICE S. ROSSI*

All of us, whether willing or not, are caught up in the current process of social change. To be sure, this is a perennial theme — so much so that, quoting some of our wits, the first of these timeworn observations that we are in a period of transition might have been articulated by Adam to Eve. Be that as it may, change today is many times more swift than that known even in recent decades. What does this fact mean for each one of us? That without our exerting the slightest personal effort, the course of our lives as American women is being shaped quite differently from that of generations in the immediate past.

In our freedom-loving democratic world, any such pronouncement has ominous implications, for fortunately, with the privilege to chart our personal lives having always been held inviolable, there is an element in most of our natures which rebels at being completely controlled by external forces. Accordingly, when tides of change sweep through our world, we must strive to find accommodation between our own lives and the new elements in our surroundings. But before we can achieve a satisfactory adjustment, it is important for us to understand the significance of the factors which are reshaping our environment.

* Alice S. Rossi, "Equality Between the Sexes: An Immodest Proposal," in *Daedalus.* The Journal of the American Academy of Arts and Sciences. XCIII, No. 2 (Spring 1964), p. 624.

The forces that are now creating new structure for the lives of American women are various and usually interdependent. Because we now benefit from improved and expanded medical services, better sanitation, and increased knowledge of nutrition, those of us in this country will have a good quarter of a century added to our lives — years for which we will be well advised to equip ourselves if the latter part of life is to have zest and significance. We are in the midst of such an explosion of knowledge that we shall have to be much better informed than those of past generations if we are not to be left hopelessly marooned in the understanding and sharing of ideas. As a consequence, education is fast becoming more widely recognized as a continuing life-long requirement both for social adjustment of the individual and labor force participation. Also, the need for skilled and creative workers in this country and abroad demands of us that we cooperate and contribute in an expanding variety of undertakings. As an example of this trend, college students, as never before, are volunteering their aid in causes for social betterment. Again, many services formerly provided by the home will be increasingly undertaken by the community — education, entertainment, care of the sick, commercial processing of foods — bringing about a radical change in the character of homemaking. For women, the significance of these conversions is that in our greatly prolonged life span we will have the chance to live more abundantly and be given a much wider choice in how we shall spend our lives.

These developments will continue to have a cumulative and profound effect upon the life patterns of American women. Collectively they will create for us the necessity of making choices. We can elect to do nothing at all about adjusting our way of living to these new social conditions and just let the forces of change bear us willy-nilly along. Or we can plan our lives to take advantage of these transformations, and our doing so will make an invaluable difference to us personally between monotony and dissatisfaction on the one hand and a well-rounded and rewarding life experience on the other.

These facts are too seldom made evident to us. Today, when a vast array of commercial interests combine in an attempt to create our self-images *for* us, we have an urgent need for cultivating awareness and critical perception in order to break through the many barriers erected to prevent girls from developing their talents and using them.

The mass media give us a commercially created image. Radio, television, popular men's and women's magazines, and advertising media present a stereotype. The successful woman is attractive, personable, eternally young, highly skilled in social relationships; is readily approachable by all those who need her help; listens intelligently; and knows how to manage a home efficiently and economically, is ruled by her emotions (except in times of crisis) rather than her intellect, and finds her personal identity only through the successes of her family. If she is above average in ability, she must be careful to conceal this. To reveal it would jeopardize her chances for marriage. — The result is a generic image of women often significantly different from what women do and are, and often significantly lacking in the womanly qualities both men and women value.[1]

This stereotype of the American woman so repetitiously presented by our mass media is a powerful deterrent to our realization that in this mid-twentieth century we are involved in one of the greatest cultural revolutions of all time, which is producing remarkable consequences in the lives of women. Even in regions of the world where for centuries little freedom and enlightenment have been known, the impact of modernization is creating for the feminine half of the population a new outlook and a new understanding of life's possibilities.

Specifically, to be an American woman today is not only to be in the forefront of this revolution, but to possess the most abundant of all opportunities for full, dynamic, and satisfying living. New frontiers have been opening for us at a constantly accelerating rate within the past two decades, and within this brief span of time a new feminine life pattern has been unfolding. The outlook of educated American women is broadening and their participation in areas of social concern and economic activity dramatically expanding. These changes are not only having a profound influence upon life patterns in the years after marriage but are altering our means of defining and maintaining values in our homes. Broadly speaking, these developments which have sometimes been termed the "second women's revolution" — the gaining of civil, political, and educational rights being the first — are bringing about for us a new understanding of ourselves and a

[1] *New Approaches to Counseling Girls in the 1960's.* A Report of the Midwest Regional Pilot Conference at University of Chicago Center for Continuing Education, February 26–27, 1965 (Washington, D.C.: Government Printing Office, 1965), p. 72.

new relationship with our families and with the communities in which we live.

A young woman may reasonably ask how such changes will affect her own future. But before we can attempt any crystal-gazing, let us remember that personal choices in life direction can be made with greater confidence and probabilities of realization when we understand the background against which they must be made. Values are often difficult to determine in periods of rapid transition, as are the means of maintaining those which we believe to have permanence. First of all then, we must gain perspective in order to understand not only where we are going, but whence we came.

Recognition of the fact that the new role of American women has been evolving since the middle of the past century is to better understand the strength of the roots through which it is nourished, as well as the necessity for making accommodations to it in our own life plans. Often, because we have not taken its background into account, the sudden acceleration of this movement within the past two decades has been a major cause for confusion in personal adjustment. We have been suffering from the cultural lag which typically follows technological transformations, for life patterns which have long been accepted are difficult to dislodge. Accordingly, even though we succeed in adapting our way of life to changing conditions, we are often plagued by unwarranted doubts, and waver in our decisions because of the disapproval of those who lack broad understanding and who cling to the older patterns in the new era.

Even a century, when viewed in longer perspective is a brief span of time in which to effect a cultural revolution as vast as that which we are now experiencing. Only forty years ago, Thomas Woody in his authoritative history of women's education in the United States had this to say:

> The education of women on a grand scale, in the United States, is of recent date; their higher education is a development of the past seventy-five years. — From the days of our primitive ancestors women have generally occupied a sheltered place and have not, therefore, received a higher cultural and professional training such as would enable them to deal with large affairs, remote from the fireside.[2]

[2] Thomas Woody, *A History of Women's Education in the United States* (New York: The Science Press, 1929), I, 1.

In fact then, until little more than one hundred years ago, the usual conception of women's social role was much like that defined by Rousseau in his *Emile* in 1792:

> Thus the whole education of women ought to be relative to men. To please them, to be useful to them, to make themselves loved and honored by them, to educate them when young, to care for them when grown, to counsel them, to console them, and to make life agreeable and sweet to them — these are the duties of women at all times and what should be taught them from infancy.[3]

What a contrast between this philosophy and that of today as shown by the fact that according to the U.S. Office of Education there were over two million women enrolled in American colleges and universities in the fall of 1964.[4] With our present almost complete acceptance of women's right to higher education, women can now study in more than nine hundred colleges and universities offering a four year course leading toward the bachelor's degree, as well as pursue advanced training for practically any profession. This sharp contrast is no more astounding than the uses women now make of their education. Whereas only a generation ago college-trained women usually thought it necessary to choose between marriage and a job, today they are most likely to marry and to seek employment too when the children are grown.[5]

It is scarcely conceivable to those of the present younger generation that in the American colonial period "there existed no real question as to the intelligence of women, it being generally accepted that they were inferior."[6] Those who received any formal intellectual training were too few to cause any significant disturbance of this conviction. Even though a woman gave the first ground on which a free school was erected in the Massachusetts Bay Colony, girls were not permitted to attend. Not until after the Revolutionary War were they allowed even on the fringes of public educational benefits in instances like that in Norwich, Connecticut, where girls were given permission to

---

[3] Jean Jacques Rousseau, *Emile,* trans. William H. Payne (New York: D. Appleton & Co., 1896), p. 263.

[4] *1965 Handbook on Women Workers* (Washington, D.C.: U.S. Women's Bureau), p. 180.

[5] Mabel Newcomer, *A Century of Higher Education for American Women* (New York: Harper & Bros., 1959), pp. 234–235.

[6] Woody, *op. cit.,* I, 92.

attend school early in the morning before the boys arrived and after they had gone home later in the day.[7]

If we recall the widespread indifference and frequent opposition to the higher education of women that prevailed even into the latter part of the nineteenth century, we can better realize the progress we have made. Woody points out that the new name, "female college," applied to Wellesley, Smith, and Mt. Holyoke, caused consternation with some and outright ridicule from others. Many thought that though college education "may have excellencies for men, — for women it can only be hardening and deforming," or that "a college curriculum would have done nothing to improve a woman's rich and beautiful mind, but only to debase it." "The publicity of a college," wrote another commentator, "must be odious to a young girl of refined and delicate feeling." Many were certain that college training would expose the physical and mental weaknesses of young women. "Alas!" bemoaned one writer, "must we crowd education upon our daughters, and, for the sake of having them 'intellectual,' make them puny, nervous, and their whole earthly existence a struggle between life and death?"

Only after a goodly number of young women had withstood the "strain" of an advanced education could such harbingers of catastrophe be convinced that the college program did not impair girls' health. The astonishing revelation to many doubting observers of that day was that college women turned out to be healthier than those who stayed at home.[8]

The very fact that such opinions now seem curious and incredible shows us how far we have come within only a century. But in another hundred years our descendants may wonder at some of the still lingering misunderstandings and prejudices about women's abilities and roles which remain with us today. Overcoming these misconceptions and making adequate use of women's talents and capabilities still present stubborn problems.

Today, we are in a period of lively controversy concerning the aims and content of women's education, but our questionings are of a different nature from those of previous decades. They relate largely to discovering ways in which we can interest a greater number of

[7] Edwin G. Dexter, *A History of Education in the United States* (New York: Macmillan Co., 1904), p. 426.

[8] Woody, *op. cit.*, II, Chap. IV.

bright young women to develop their full talents and abilities through college training and maintain a competence for life-long use of their education.

The number of women enrolling in college for the first time relative to the number graduating from high school has increased almost steadily since 1948. However, a comparison of the number of men first-time college enrollees with the number of high school graduates indicates that a much higher proportion of men than of women went on to college throughout the period 1948 to 1964. Trends in comparisons at the doctoral level are also interesting. In 1900, 6 per cent of all doctoral degrees were earned by women. In 1920 the proportion had risen to a peak of 15 per cent, in 1950 had dropped to a low of 9 per cent with an upswing to 11 per cent in 1964.[9] Of the 421,000 girls sixteen to twenty-one years of age who had left college as of 1963, 23 per cent gave marriage and pregnancy as their main reason and 13 per cent gave economic factors. Although the U.S. Office of Education notes an increased holding power of our public schools in the past five years, the drop-out rate for girls there also remains high. Forty per cent of the drop-outs gave marriage or pregnancy as the reason for leaving school (37.8 per cent for whites, 48.8 per cent for non-whites). Additionally, over 18 per cent said they were not interested in school.[10] Many of these girls, when they reach their late thirties, will discover that they are not prepared to enter the sort of paid employment which will then be attractive to them.

It is somewhat encouraging to know that during the past decade college enrollments for women have increased proportionately more than for men, yet far too large a percentage of women who enroll in college do not finish. One factor in this situation is that, even to date, our society has not thought a college education as important for girls as for boys. Over and above their educational need for entering paid employment, a serious consequence of this short-sightedness is that we have failed to make our daughters understand the importance of education in their roles as mothers, from whom their children will receive the beginnings of their education. But of even more serious consequence is the fact that we have not sufficiently recognized a woman's personal need for education, especially in the later years of

[9] *Trends in Educational Attainment of Women* (Washington, D.C.: U.S. Women's Bureau, June 1966), pp. 4, 8.

[10] *1965 Handbook on Women Workers, op. cit.,* pp. 178–180.

her greatly lengthened life span when she is largely freed from family responsibilities and has time to enjoy the fruits of her education and to make a still fuller contribution to society. The United States Department of Labor estimates that by the year 1970 over half of the women in the 45–54 year age group and almost half of those in the 35–44 year group will work. They will need education to hold good jobs and to become contributing citizens.

The purpose and timing of higher education within the feminine life span are other factors to which we are now giving thought. What sort of training best meets the needs of most middle-class women? Shall it be in the liberal arts, in a vocation, or in both? For the woman who marries and enters a career later in her life, would it not be best for her to receive a liberal education before her marriage and the greater part of her vocational or professional training in the post-family years just before she enters a career, or re-enters one for a longer period? These are questions to be answered by professional educators and by young women themselves in planning their lives. The new thinking about these matters grows out of changes in the modern feminine life pattern characterized by early and nearly universal marriage, the growing trend toward work outside the home, and especially entering a profession again, or for the first time, when the children are older.[11] The United States Department of Labor predicts that these trends will continue.

In women's progress toward fuller self-realization, the decade following World War II appears to have had special significance. In this period a century of growing discontent with a limited domestic role burst into open rebellion, and out of this decade of frustration was to grow in the 1960's a more positive approach to the problem. In the immediate post-war years educated women sensed as never before that they had capabilities far greater than were being entirely used in the traditional feminine role. The result during the 1950's was a decade of literature expressing futility. The American woman did not always understand why she felt so suddenly rebellious, and many who voiced the feminine protest were afflicted with a sense of guilt that home, husband, and children did not satisfy their longings for more complete self-realization. Sidney J. Levy in an essay on "The Meanings of Work" has captured the feeling of women of this period in these ironic words:

11 Mabel Newcomer, *op. cit.,* p. 248.

Chart I. Women in the Labor Force by Age, 1890, 1940, 1956, 1965

Per Cent in
Labor Force

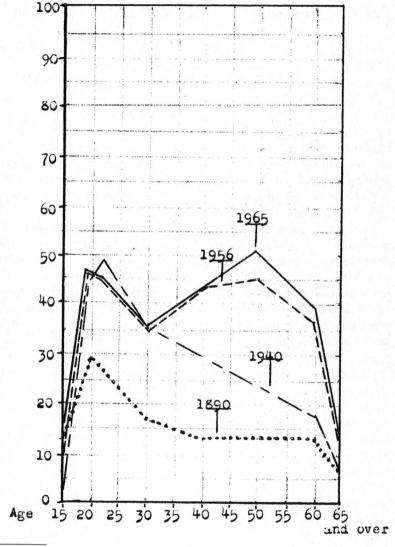

Adapted from National Manpower Council, *Womanpower*. Data from *U.S. Census: Current Population Reports*.

Meanwhile, back in the kitchen is another person. She does not work. Life requires of her merely that she cook, launder, and dust, mop, diaper, and scrub. She manages an establishment of more or less unruly personnel, only one of whom did she interview prior to accepting. She is purchasing agent, finance officer, processor of raw materials, and public relations council. But she is called "just a housewife."[12]

This expression of feminine frustration, so characteristic of the 1950's, is concluded with the comment "how a woman interprets her work reflects how she defines herself as a woman within the limits of social boundaries."

It is because of the extension of these social boundaries today that the feeling of futility is being replaced by a sense of excitement and challenge. Although the present-day woman is still exposed to numerous lingering expressions of frustration, some of them having great popular appeal,* she is beginning to realize that her chances for self-fulfillment are no longer so limited if she has sufficient education, sense of direction, and a will to achieve.

That American women are seeking a larger sphere of participation is apparent from Chart I. Here we see that the number of women working outside their homes in 1890 declines steadily after age twenty. In contrast to this, in 1956 and 1965 a decline in employment takes place between the ages of eighteen and thirty, with a sharp rise again between thirty and forty, and a continued gradual rise until age fifty. Moreover, after about age thirty the percentage of employment remains at a consistently higher level to the end of the employment span in 1956 and 1965 than in either 1890 or 1940.[13]

This changed picture of employment has immense importance for women's educational needs. It means that women must have not only liberal education to develop them as whole persons, but training in a skill which will provide them with a means for greater social usefulness throughout their greatly lengthened span of years.

---

* See Betty Friedan, *The Feminine Mystique* (New York: Dell Publishing Co., Inc., 1964.)

12 Sidney J. Levy, quotation from "The Meaning of Work," published by the Center for the Study of Liberal Education for Adults in *Education and a Woman's Life* (Washington, D.C.: 1963), Foreword.

13 National Manpower Council, *Womanpower* (New York: Columbia University Press, 1957), p. 307.

CHAPTER 2

Exchanging Old Life Patterns for New

Some girls decide early in life that they want to concentrate on a specific field of study and work. For most, however, plans about future activities are not clearly defined and eventually may be decided much more by chance than by personal choice.*

It is important that we see the new life and work patterns of American women in broad social context. The new self-image which has been so rapidly emerging since the Second World War cannot be correctly understood if viewed as an isolated development, but must be interpreted as an outgrowth of the many revolutionary transformations occurring in our society.

With our recent progress in science having been so dramatic that we frequently claim to have wrought more changes within the past fifty years than in the previous five hundred, we are now becoming acutely aware of the consequences of these developments upon our individual lives and upon our social relationships. For educated women, the result has been a vigorous attempt to attain a clearer understanding of their own capabilities as well as of their social potential. For society as a whole, the effect has been an aroused conscience about equality of opportunity for women and a greater awareness of the potential usefulness of feminine abilities in building a better society. As stated by Margaret Mead, there has been "a profound and growing unease among those who felt an important part of American

---

* From *Job Horizons for College Women in the 1960's,* Women's Bureau, U.S. Department of Labor (Washington, D.C., 1964), p. 1.

11

democracy to be the freedom of women to contribute to our society not only as mothers, but also as individuals."[1]

The significance of this development in the lives of women was concisely summarized by Dag Hammarskjold in his address at the Eighth Session of the United Nations Commission on the Status of Women:

> Among all the achievements of the past century, including those discoveries and developments that have transformed the lives of men and altered the meaning of time and space, it may be doubted whether any is so profoundly significant and in the long run so beneficial as the emancipation of women.[2]

What does the crystal ball reveal about the life prospects of modern young women? Fully ninety per cent of present-day college undergraduates will marry and have a family, usually interrupting the beginning of a professional or business career. Because of the present trend of early marriages, they will be on the average only thirty-two years old when the youngest child reaches school age.[3] Since the present life expectancy for white women* is 74.6 years,[4] they will have forty years of life ahead of them after the youngest child enters school. The average college girl today will probably spend twenty-five years in paid employment.[5] Statistics also show that most women will outlive their husbands, making it additionally advisable for them to have means of being self-reliant.

The recent phenomenal extension of the duration of life creates at once problems and a challenge. Gordon W. Blackwell, when Chancellor of Woman's College of the University of North Carolina, had in mind the present long span of women's lives following the early child-rearing period when he asked his students, "What will

---

* Non-white women have 67.2 years expectancy.

[1] Margaret Mead, Introduction to *American Women*. The Report of the President's Commission on the Status of Women (New York: Charles Scribner's Sons, 1965), p. 4.

[2] Dag Hammarskjold in *United Nations Bulletin*, XVI (April 1, 1954), p. 249.

[3] Paul C. Glick, "The Life Cycle of the Family," *Marriage and Family Living*, XVII, No. 1 (February, 1955), 3.

[4] U.S. Bureau of the Census, *Statistical Abstract of the United States*. 87th edition. (Washington, D.C., 1966), p. 53.

[5] "What's Next for the Girl Who Graduates from High School?" Pamphlet. (University of Indiana, 1960).

these forty years be like? How will you use them?"[6] Women can no longer think in terms of an early marriage as their ultimate and exclusive objective, as did earlier generations. The necessity of planning for the gift of added years is a concept which those now in high school and college must come to accept. As anthropologists are now pointing out, never have American women lived so long; yet, when young, they are so little concerned with thinking ahead toward preparing themselves for this lengthened life.

The relative newness of this situation can be more clearly understood by comparing the present life expectancy for women with that in the middle of the past century. In 1850, women had an average life expectancy of only 40.5 years, outliving their husbands by 2.2 years. Even as late as the turn of the century they could expect to live only 50.7 years, 2.8 years longer than their husbands. In other words, during approximately the past hundred years, women's average life expectancy has increased about thirty-four years, and the differential between the average length of women's lives and that of their husbands' from 2.2 to 6.9 years.[7]

But of equal significance with the greatly increased longevity is the fact that, because of advances in public health and nutrition, women will have better health and resources of energy to live younger lives. While a century ago a woman was elderly at fifty, today she is still enjoying the prime of her life at that age, and her daughters will probably be in even better health. With modern technology to aid her, and the increase in community services benefiting the home — trained nursing care, antibiotics, commercially prepared foods, outside entertainment — she will have much more time available for living these added years.

A distinct characteristic of a modern woman's life pattern closely related to the lengthening of the life span is the division of her years into segments. It is as if she has several different lives in the course of one. There are first the years of formal schooling in which she will usually receive some preparation for occupational competence outside the home. These are followed by a very short period in paid employment. She next experiences the more confining period of child-rearing, and finally the much longer span of years in which she will probably

[6] Gordon W. Blackwell, "What We Are About." Pamphlet. (Public Relations Department, University of North Carolina at Greensboro, 1959).

[7] *Statistical Abstract, op. cit.*, p. 53.

return to paid or voluntary employment outside the home. Each of these three stages has a distinct character, contrasting sharply with the others in occupational orientation and emotional involvement. A woman's problem here is to find coherence among them.

We cite this lack of coherence among the several stages of modern women's lives as a relatively new situation because, except for widows, such shifts of direction seldom occurred for married women of a century ago and even much later. In past generations, when a woman's life was much shorter and her education more limited, the period of transition following the rearing of her own children was eased by her later years of grandmotherhood, which were relatively consistent with her way of life as a mother. The present mobility of our population and the consequent geographical separation of younger from older generations has, of course, also been largely contributive to disrupting this older pattern.

To date, formal education has done little to help the modern woman achieve this much needed coherence in her life. Today's education is geared to schooling girls, along with their male classmates, for the man's world of competitive achievement without teaching them to anticipate the shifts of direction and varying needs during the later segments of the life experience. Shortly following a four-year college training, and today often before that, a girl is plunged into the role of wife and mother, where too often she learns that she has not been psychologically prepared for the transition. Now she must play an extroverted role. At this point, she is likely to feel that any professional interest which her formal education may have fostered must be at least temporarily surrendered in service to her family. She has no sooner achieved this very different orientation than a second period of adjustment arrives when the children leave home. The difficulties accompanying this latter transition are likely to be two-fold. There will have to be a considerable adjustment in her emotional attachments, and, at the same time, if she has allowed the preceding years to restrict her so narrowly to domesticity that her professional and cultural interests have been almost totally neglected, she will have difficulty making a satisfying use of her greater leisure. Consequently, she will find her opportunities for reemployment limited in comparison with her innate abilities and early training. Confusion with regard to an integrated purpose throughout the total life span is frequently the result.

Thus, a major development of this century, which would appear to have a relationship both with the lengthening life span and with the fragmentation of the women's traditional role, is the phenomenal increase in women's employment outside the home. Our modern, more youthful mothers and grandmothers are seeking paid jobs, and many of them continuing, or entering for the first time, professional careers. This trend in itself does not seem to imply that they value their homes less, but usually that their employment, which is either economically necessary or used to improve the family's standard of living, serves to maintain an adequate level of purpose in their lives. For it is becoming increasingly possible, except when the children are young, to combine home duties with some kind of outside job.

To evaluate this growing trend, we turn to estimates by the United States Department of Labor, showing comparisons between the rate of women's employment today and that rate in preceding decades. In 1920, only 23 per cent of the women fourteen years old and over were in the labor force in contrast to 37 per cent in 1964.[8] Moreover, since the turn of the century there has been a continuous rise in the median (half above/half below) age of women workers. In 1900 it was twenty-six years; in 1945, thirty-four years; and in 1965, forty-one years compared with forty years for men workers.[9]

The U.S. Department of Labor points out that with increasingly larger numbers of women expected to enter the labor force in the coming decade, the trend appears not to be a temporary phenomenon. It is anticipated that between 1964 and 1980, the number of women workers will probably show a rise of 41 per cent as compared with 27 per cent for men[10] (Table 1). A larger proportion of older women will work. Professional, office, and sales jobs are now growing the fastest, and the biggest increase is occurring in occupations requiring the most education and training,[11] with the result that education will receive ever increasing emphasis in the decade ahead (Chart II). The employment of married women will be further facilitated if the Department of Labor's estimate of the increase in part-time jobs

[8] *1965 Handbook on Women Workers* (U.S. Women's Bureau Bulletin No. 290 [Washington, D.C., 1966]), p. 221.

[9] *Ibid.*, p. 12.

[10] *Ibid.*, p. 221.

[11] *Manpower Challenge of the 1960's* (U.S. Department of Labor Publication [Washington, D.C., 1960]), p. 11.

Table 1. Labor-Force Participation Rates, by Sex and by Age of Women, 1964 and Projected to 1980[1]

(Persons 14 years of age and over)

Sex and Age	Actual 1964	Projected 1970	Projected 1975	Projected 1980
Total	56.5	57.5	57.8	58.3
Men	77.2	77.0	76.9	77.2
Women	37.0	39.1	39.9	40.6
14 to 19 years	28.1	30.1	30.6	31.0
20 to 24 years	49.2	50.3	51.5	52.6
25 to 34 years	37.1	38.6	39.3	40.3
35 to 44 years	44.8	47.5	49.0	50.0
45 to 54 years	51.0	55.3	57.6	59.5
55 to 64 years	39.8	43.8	45.7	47.3
55 to 59 years	45.9	51.5	54.2	56.2
60 to 64 years	32.7	34.8	36.2	37.3
65 years and over	9.6	9.8	9.8	9.9
65 to 69 years	16.2	17.4	17.4	17.4
70 years and over	5.8	5.9	6.0	6.1
18 to 64 years	44.4	47.2	48.2	49.0

Source: *1965 Handbook on Women Workers*, U.S. Women's Bureau Bulletin 290, based on "Manpower Report of the President and a Report on Manpower Requirements, Resources, Utilization and Training by the U.S. Department of Labor." March 1965.

[1] Annual averages.

Chart II. **Percent Change in Employment 1960–1970**

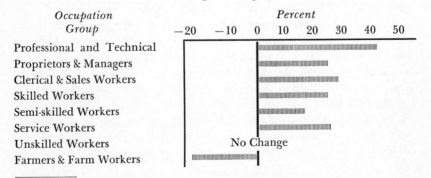

Source: U.S. Department of Labor, *Manpower Challenge of the 1960's.*

materializes. Sixteen million persons are expected to be part-time workers by 1970, a 30 per cent increase over 1960.[12] Are capable girls looking far enough ahead to plan not only for a brief period of employment, then marriage, but for this long period of employment later in their lives? Unfortunately, the answer to this question is not too encouraging when only one out of four young women capable of doing college work go on to college, and so many others drop out after a year or two. Unless there can be a reversal of this trend, it means that a comparatively much larger proportion of women than men will be in relatively unskilled jobs, making the women's employment picture less bright in spite of increase in numbers.

Although we here have a special interest in how paid employment is affecting the life patterns of women themselves, an equally great change should be noted in the character of the homes they create. An entirely new form of family life is emerging, characterized by new methods of work performance and closer contacts with the community. In the homes of yesterday, which were more nearly self-sufficient economic units, the housewife played a more important role in production of goods. She was usually content through this function to have status with her family and neighbors solely by the skilled and efficient management of her household. It was quite enough for her to excel in maintaining the cleanliness and orderliness of her house, performing household tasks efficiently, creating the family wardrobe with her own hands, baking the best cakes for the church bazaar, and perhaps writing a paper for the literary club.

Homes of today are less self-sufficient; they are far more reliant upon the community. With the advances in technology which have increased community services benefiting the home, housewives of the middle class have found that many useful tasks which they previously performed for their families are no longer necessary. As intelligent women, especially those who are college-trained, now better realize that housekeeping extends beyond their doormat, greater numbers are informing themselves on community issues and, through their organizations, having an ever larger influence in community affairs. By helping to shape their environment, they have an influence on the home. We know that such miscellaneous but important concerns as pure water and pure foods, excellent schools, control of contagion, taxes and

---

[12] *Ibid.,* p. 19.

tariffs, political elections, adult education, cultural opportunities, and the maintenance of international peace, to mention only a few, have a direct bearing upon the welfare of our homes.

The present close interrelatedness of home and community has exerted a new influence on ways of rearing our children. As the child matures, the mother recognizes the values in the orientation of the child's interests toward the community. Freed from much of the mechanics of operating a household, she has more time to devote to the socialization of her children. Too true, as we have often had it pointed out to us, a whole new flood of duties has rushed in upon the modern housewife to consume the time and energy saved her by new household conveniences. She may bemoan that minutes economized by the electric dishwasher are spent in taxiing children to school, lessons, and play centers; or that time saved by drip-dry clothing is dissipated by attending a PTA meeting. But are these very facts not symbolic of the growing socialization of the home? Many of the tasks which typified the former family self-sufficiency are replaced by those which now give that family closer contacts with the community. David Riesman points out additionally that today "parents, fearing to be over-protective, do not hang on to their children, but energetically facilitate their social contacts outside the home."[13]

Furthermore, community orientation is as imperative a need for the woman herself as for her children, as she will come to realize even more fully in the long second half of her life. As Lynn White remarks, "Unless a sense of participating in the community saturates the home, it becomes a prison in which the soul withers."[14] The older woman's need for this relationship has lately increased because children are now weaned from dependence on their parental homes early in life, and eventually move to distant locations from which contacts with parents become less frequent. Gone for most people are the days when several related families lived self-sufficently within the radius of a few town blocks. Today, a mother in Cleveland may have children living in San Diego or Singapore.

The promotion of the growth of the social conscience is peculiarly a mark of our twentieth century higher education to which many younger women are responding with their own special contributions

---

[13] David Riesman, "Women: Their Orbits and Their Education," *Journal of the American Association of University Women, LI*, No. 2 (January, 1958), 79.

[14] Lynn White, Jr., *Educating Our Daughters* (New York: Harper & Bros., 1950), p. 104.

to social needs. In the pioneering decades of higher education for women, social responsibility was not the main emphasis. In contrast today, as James Bryant Conant has said, "Education for citizenship represents the modern approach to education."[15] This is especially true of those for whom a college education has aroused a social conscience and a realization of all the possibilities for life's fulfillment and enrichment. The lengthened life span, better health, lessening of household drudgery, education, better working conditions outside the home, widening opportunities for both paid and voluntary services in the community — all these factors are creating a new perspective for middle-class American women. And it is this class that sets the standards for others.

Many are asking if these new life patterns are in the best interests of the home. Certainly there is ample evidence that homemaking is still the chief occupation of American women. A significant and gratifying factor in the molding of these new life patterns is that the married woman's holding a job during part of her life span does not seem to detract from her interest in her home and the values traditionally ascribed to it. The great majority have shown by their behavior in recent decades that they cherish their role as wife and mother far above the role of wage earner. In fact, it is difficult to persuade girls during their high school and college years to look beyond their goals of marriage and family, and so to plan in accordance with their full capabilities for those segments of their lives in which they will eventually find themselves interested in employment outside the home. Statistics show that as the proportion of women in paid employment has risen, the average age for marriage has decreased and the birth rate has sharply risen. Simultaneously, a smaller proportion of women has remained single. In most instances the presence or lack of young children in the home determines the woman's availability in the labor market. Most women wait until their children are in school before they return to work, and mothers of small children who work are usually employed part-time, during part of the day or for part of the year. Although married women work for a variety of reasons, the strongest motive seems to be to add to the total income so that they can improve the standard of living for their families.[16]

[15] James Bryant Conant, *Education in a Divided World* (Cambridge: Harvard University Press, 1949), p. 75.

[16] Robert Smuts, *Women and Work in America* (New York: Columbia University Press, 1959), pp. 147–148.

The changes in self-image and life patterns have, of course, brought with them problems of social adjustment, an inevitable consequence of the fact that these newer concepts of women's role are in sharp contrast with those held only twenty years ago. In the days when the feminist influence was still strong and before the extensive mechanization of household tasks, most women believed that the only possibility open to them was to choose between marriage or a career. Since World War II, the accepted pattern is becoming, not *either-or,* but *both.* Most college-trained women are now finding it possible to have both a family and a job, either paid or voluntary, at some time during their lives. Whereas, historically, women first attained the option of choice *between marriage and career,* today their choice is *among careers* which they can certainly combine with marriage. It is probably reasonable to anticipate that the lag in public understanding which is accompanying this marked change in women's life patterns will in time yield both to a more universal acceptance of the pattern and to a more ordered and integrated design for women's lives.

Although we are here specifically concerned with observing the process of change in the self-image for wives and mothers, we cannot overlook in passing the fact that these developments have, of course, a corresponding effect upon the role of men, particularly with respect to the exercise of authority in family decisions and division of labor in the home. The effect of these changes upon the role of men is a matter about which we have insufficient data at present. Nothing is known yet about male evaluations, and Blood states that the impact of the wife's employment on the couple's appraisal of their marriage is not yet understood,[17] although Nye suggests the possibility that the marital adjustment may be adversely affected if the wife earns more than the husband.[18] The two sociologists, Blood and Hamblin, conclude from their study comparing marriages involving working wives with those of non-working wives that the woman's employment usually results in a more equalitarian ideology for the wife, but that she does not use her economic contribution to the family to gain greater authority at the expense of her husband. They observe that these husbands and wives are more likely to assume equal responsibility in decision-making, as well as to arrange the division of labor

[17] Robert O. Blood, "The Husband-Wife Relationship," in Nye and Hoffman, *The Employed Mother in America* (Chicago: Rand McNally Co., 1963), p. 304.
[18] F. Ivan Nye, "Marital Interaction," *Ibid.,* p. 280.

in household tasks according to the availability of one or the other.[19]

Other authorities agree that the changes in sex roles seem to be quite consistently toward equalitarianism, especially among families of the middle class and those of higher educational attainments. One writer points out that with the spread of education to ever greater numbers we can expect this concept to become even more prevalent.[20] Such a development is probably a counterpart of another tendency, independent of employment patterns, in the husband-wife relationship — away from traditional authoritarianism on the part of the husband and towards companionship in marriage. One study points to the seemingly less sharp distinctions between our customary concepts of the "exclusively masculine" and the "exclusively feminine," and to a gradual convergence of the sex roles taking place in our society.[21]

In 1955, Florence Kluckhohn, associate in the Laboratory of Social Relations, Harvard University, commented, "To me, the serious problem in the family structure of the United States is defining masculine and feminine roles in such a way as to let us break through the tendency toward segregation, and have a more satisfying husband-wife relationship."[22] Perhaps young couples are already making a beginning toward a solution of this problem. On the one hand, earnings from the young wife's employment before the arrival of children make it possible for her husband to raise his educational sights and thus advance himself professionally. On the other hand, his sharing in the operation and responsibility of the household makes possible for his wife a larger participation in the community. In any event, where such reciprocity exists, some benefits must surely result for both husband and wife, as well as for the children. Certainly, each partner is given fuller insight into the other's problems and interests, and women have gained a wider scope for developing their full potentialities.

In summary, two major concepts emerge from these situations and attitudes affecting the modern woman's understanding of herself.

[19] Robert Blood and Robert Hamblin, "The Effect of the Wife's Employment on the Family Power Structure," *Social Forces*, XXXVI (May, 1958), 347–352.

[20] Ruth Hartley, "Some Implications of Current Sex-Role Patterns," *Merrill-Palmer Quarterly of Behavior and Development,* VI (1959–1960), 153–164.

[21] Donald Brown, "Sex-Role Development in a Changing Culture," *Psychological Bulletin, LIV,* No. 4 (July, 1958). Reprint.

[22] Florence Kluckhohn in *The Effective Use of Womanpower* (U.S. Women's Bureau Publication No. 257 [Washington, D.C., 1955]), p. 19.

She must foresee her life as divided into distinct, though overlapping segments — the periods of formal education, of child-rearing, of community service. In contrast with women of the past century and the beginning of this, she must plan for an education which will open to her greater opportunities to develop her *total* potentialities as an individual — to become a whole person, to live a far more abundant life.

Inseparable from this concept is a second one — a woman's need to integrate the several parts of her life. David Riesman has said, "There is a growing feeling of young people that they want what Erick Fromm calls 'relatedness,' rather than bits and pieces in their lives. They are eager to be shown — shown meanings, connections and purposes beyond themselves."[23] Many leading educators are deeply concerned with helping students find "that purpose beyond themselves" and establish a sense of unity for their lives. These educators know that the discovery of richer basic values, essential to a sense of fulfillment, will do more than help women achieve success in each stage of their life experience — that sufficient and well chosen values can bind the purpose of each segment of their lives to the others and ease what might otherwise be an abrupt and frustrating, even a painful, transition.

As Kate Hevner Mueller of Indiana University, a scholar much concerned with women's education, points out: "The pattern, the pressure, is inescapable. The college woman — , as all other young women, needs, wants, and plans to have a husband, a home, a family, and some kind of a job. Educators must not only catch up with her but overtake her and help her to learn both the attitudes and the skills that will give her the best possible experience in all of these."[24] While the problem for our institutions of learning is to provide women with an education that is sufficient for modern needs, the concern for young women themselves must be that they take a longer and more realistic view of their futures and develop their *total* individual capabilities for use in the several segments of their greatly lengthened life span, and think about an integrating purpose for the whole of it.

[23] Riesman, *op. cit.*, p. 80.
[24] Kate H. Mueller, "The Cultural Pressures on Women," in *Education of Women — Signs for the Future* (American Council on Education Publication [Washington, D.C., 1958]), p. 56.

CHAPTER 3

Factors Shaping the Modern Woman's Life Pattern

*To appreciate the larger phenomenon of the massive move-
ment of mothers into the labor force, we must consider the
rapid and fundamental social and cultural developments
which have changed America.*

F. Ivan Nye and Lois Wladis Hoffman*

If, in anticipating her future, a young woman plans to enter the
labor market at some time after her marriage, possibly in her middle
or late thirties when her children are older, can she be certain of occupational opportunities? Assuming that a full employment condition
is maintained and that economic growth continues, she can be reasonably sure of such opportunities. Granted these assurances, can she also
count on the present trend in women's employment continuing? A
glance at this trend since the turn of the century will persuade her
that it is not a temporary phenomenon (Table 2). It will be seen
that the rate of women's employment has risen from 18 per cent of
all women in 1890 to 28 per cent in 1940 to 37 per cent in 1965. To
be further convinced of the stability of women's newly emerging life
patterns, we should view them against the background of other social
transformations within the past century which have helped produce
them.

What are these forces which have so greatly affected women's traditional role? Is the seeking of paid employment by such a large per-

* F. Ivan Nye and Lois Wladis Hoffman, *The Employed Mother in America*
(Chicago: Rand McNally & Co., 1963), p. 3.

Table 2. **Women in the Labor Force (Selected years)**

Year	Women workers (14 years and over)		
	Number	Per cent of all workers	Per cent of all women
Recent Highlights[1]			
April 1965	26,139,000	35	37
April 1962	24,052,000	34	36
Start of Sixties (April 1960)	23,239,000	33	36
Mid-fifties (April 1955)	20,154,000	31	34
Korean War (April 1953)	19,296,000	31	33
Pre-Korea (April 1950)	18,063,000	29	32
Post-war (April 1947)	16,320,000	28	30
World War II (April 1945)	19,570,000	36	37
Pre-World War II (March 1940)	13,840,000	25	28
Long Term Trends[2]			
1930 (April)	10,396,000	22	24
1920 (January)	8,229,000	20	23
1900 (June)	4,999,000	18	20
1890 (June)	3,704,000	17	18

Source: U.S. Department of Labor, Bureau of Labor Statistics; and U.S. Department of Commerce, Bureau of the Census.

[1] "Current Population Reports" for civilian labor force.
[2] Decennial census for total labor force, including Armed Forces.

centage of American women an outgrowth of the women's rights campaigns of previous decades? The rights crusade and its effect upon women's status have been so widely publicized that we are often inclined to overlook other less obvious but more basic causes. The efforts of the feminists were sustained by our national economic growth and the democratic idealism of the western world.

In fact, since the close of World War I the strength of feminist idealism in America and some European countries has been rapidly waning. It has been a matter of considerable comment that in present-day America the movement of women into paid employment seems to be in avoidance of any ideological principle. Carl Degler comments that today "women shun like a disease any feminist ideology," and he finds an element of proof for this statement in the fact that American women have been more interested in jobs than careers.[1] It is, indeed, interesting to note that, as the nineteenth century feminists were criticized for their ideological aggressiveness, the modern American woman is often found fault with for handicapping her progress through lack of it.

Although feminism has made its contribution to the American woman's improved status, many conditions are operative in shaping her present life pattern over which women themselves have had little control. These influences are to be found in our economic growth, which has created a need for women in paid employment; in work mechanization, which has increased the number of jobs to which women are physically adapted; in generally better working conditions; in a new psychological need of women; and in our social philosophy.

Although the greater number and variety of work opportunities is usually cited as a major factor in drawing women into the labor force, closely related to this cause are the changes in work performance, kinds of work, and social classification of those who work. For the following facts associated with these changes the author has drawn upon the research by Robert W. Smuts of Columbia University.[2]

The modern woman is not so much experiencing a greater load of work than her predecessors, but rather a change in kind and conditions of work. The shift in the setting for certain kinds of work from the home to the factory has too often obscured our memory of the fact that women's labor in other areas beside housekeeping until comparatively recent years has been part of her traditional role. Women have always been employed in producing goods for the family; the difference is that goods and services which were formerly supplied by them at home *without* pay are now produced by them outside the home *for* pay. Looking back on the lives of our grandmothers, we may well wonder how they managed to do so much in the production of goods to supply family needs.

In historical perspective, the domestic production of many consumer goods in a once more rural America occurred until a comparatively recent date. As late as 1890 nearly half of all American women lived

[1] Carl N. Degler, "The Changing Place of Women in America," *Daedalus,* Spring 1964, XCIII, No. 2 (Proceedings of the American Academy of Arts and Sciences), 663.

[2] Robert W. Smuts, *Women and Work in America* (New York: Columbia University Press, 1959), pp. 66–83.

on farms, and in some regions frontier conditions still existed. But even in the more settled farming areas of that day, the work-day was from sun-up to sun-down and often later. The number of jobs performed by housewives in this period staggers the modern imagination. It included making all the clothing for women and children in the family, and not only processing most of the food but raising it in the family garden. Milking, churning, and gathering eggs were regularly recurring chores. Sheets were hemmed and curtains and bed coverings made at home, as well as soap and sometimes mattresses and floor coverings. Canning of fruits and vegetables for the winter months was a time-consuming task. Eggs and butter not needed by the family were taken to town by the housewife to trade for the few items not produced at home, or sold to have money for other household necessities. Time was required for still other duties such as feeding and watering livestock, and pumping and hauling water from the well for drinking, cooking, bathing, and laundering. With the lack of modern medicines and knowledge of nutrition, sicknesses were more frequent and of longer duration. Nursing was done at home, and calls to help sick neighbors were frequent.

Even as late as the early twentieth century, women remained the home producers of many consumer goods, but the coming of the factory foretold a widespread change in this pattern of work performance. With the shift of population from farms to cities, food and clothing formerly produced at home were replaced by those which were factory-made. However, many customs of the farm were at first carried over into city living so that at the turn of the century women's work to supply family needs was certainly not much eased by moving to more densely populated areas. Wives no longer had men at home during the day to help with household chores. While husbands and sons worked away from home for ten or twelve hours a day, six days a week, wives were still working almost as many hours a day as they did on the farm to supply family necessities. Except where living was too crowded, houses still had their garden plots and poultry which women tended, and fruit and vegetable yields to be home processed. Moreover, all of these chores were performed without today's electric and gas appliances, city water, and central heating. Being deprived of money from the sale of surplus dairy products, many women in less favorable circumstances made clothing for other families or took in boarders. There can be little doubt that wives in the late nineteenth and early twentieth centuries were as much producers of goods and services for their families as today's married women in paid employment.

However, the revolution in women's work was soon to follow (the change in men's work patterns had occurred with the change to urban living), as factory-processed foods, ready-made clothing, and commercial laundry services were introduced. These developments, together with the invention of labor-saving devices benefiting the home — sewing and washing machines, vacuum cleaners, refrigerators, central heating, and city water supplies — gave women time and opportunity to work outside the home and to work for pay.

Aside from the economic advantages of paid employment, two little understood factors of a psychological nature have been important in attracting women into places of business. As the factory system removed the production of goods from the home, it also impaired that part of women's purpose which was formerly expressed in creative manual work. There is not only therapeutic value in physical work but satisfaction in being able to see and measure the results of one's output. As we have already noted, to excel in the making of clothing and home furnishings and in the preparation of foods was once a sufficient source of immediate gratification and pride for the housewife. This part of her purpose destroyed, she began to seek new direction for these satisfactions in paid employment.

Furthermore, with places of work separated from places of living, women's social needs were not satisfied. In work on the farm, women had worked beside men. Production of goods, maintenance of the home, and care of children had been an enterprise in which husband and wife had cooperated. Although work was strenuous, companionship was constant. In the new city environment, where places of business were distant from home and neighbors were most often strangers to each other, women were deprived of adult companionship during the entire workday.

So the mechanization of the home and the factory production of home commodities, which so enormously reduced expenditures of time and energy, deprived women of psychic satisfactions formerly resulting from companionship and creative manual work. This factor has been largely influential in promoting women's interest in paid employment, which again provides wives adult companionship during the workday and the satisfaction of receiving a paycheck with which to purchase, instead of make, commodities for the home. Paid employment became a new way to give their families a higher standard of living.

Viewed in perspective, the entrance of married women into the labor market is a resumption by them of part of the economic support of the family which they have historically shared. It is only within the past century that American women have been freed from their share of this responsibility while their husbands have been given the entire burden. Now, in the mid-twentieth century their economic function is being restored, and the wife again assumes a share of economic support.

Furthering the women-to-work movement has been the change in types of paid work, which in turn has affected the social class characteristics of the women who work. Better pay has also helped to bring about this result. In the late nineteenth century, most of the jobs for women were in unskilled or semi-skilled factory employment, of which the textile mills offered the most opportunities. A married woman worked only in event of her husband's death, disability, or inability to provide enough for family subsistence. Today, in contrast to this situation, the sharpest increase in women's paid employment is occurring among the well-educated and well-to-do middle class and in the professional fields. Women are admitted to almost all professional schools, and people no longer believe that it is disgraceful for a woman to want a job or a career.

Vast improvements in conditions of work are also a significant factor in the acceptance of paid jobs among the higher income groups. It is difficult today for us to imagine the conditions that existed in the 1890's and even later. Work was most strenuous, and the wearying effect of a twelve-hour workday was increased by noise, bad smells, extreme heat and humidity from factory processes, lack of ventilation, and dangerous work conditions. With few exceptions, employers took no interest in their employees and were completely indifferent to correcting intolerable conditions. Machinery was not equipped with safety devices, so that accidents were not uncommon.

Even in the more skilled jobs, conditions were hard. Private nurses were on duty twenty-four hours a day, seven days a week; and before the establishment of nursing schools, unsanitary, even vermin-infested, hospitals made a nurse's duties both revolting and hazardous to her own health. The urban teacher was almost the only one who enjoyed comparatively good working conditions. But as late as 1910, eighty per cent of the teaching jobs in this country were in one-room, one-teacher schools where conditions were far from easy and discipline often presented almost insuperable problems. Office work did not, of course, involve as much physical strain as some other jobs, but a clerk or book-keeper was likely to be the only woman in the office, and the rooms were dark, unventilated, and usually filled with the stench of tobacco. The office job, however, did attract a somewhat higher class of women, for most typists had received more education than women in other pursuits.

The extremely low wages paid to women also contributed to the poor esteem in which working women were held by those in higher income brackets. In factories women's wages were about half that of men's, and women in all jobs were paid much less.

Today, improvements both in conditions and in pay have been brought about by federal and state laws governing standards of safety, comfort, cleanliness, and wages. Mechanization, of course, has also been a powerful factor in making work more desirable by sharply decreasing the number of workers in production of goods and making available many more openings of a white-collar variety, such as those in designing, management, and educational, recreational and other kinds of services.

Along with these results of the industrial revolution, a specific influence was at work to increase the restlessness of married women and compel them to seek broader interests outside the boundaries of their homes. That influence was education. At the time when many were moving from farms to cities, the rights campaigns were opening far greater educational opportunities for women. Many of our most illustrious women's colleges trace their origins to the latter part of the nineteenth century. In the same period, colleges and universities that had provided education only for men began opening their doors to women. This broadening of educational opportunities among the upper and middle classes extended women's cultural interests and social outlook. The result was a movement which projected their activities into the wider orbit outside their homes. Women's clubs were formed as an expression of this widened interest in cultural pursuits, and church missionary organizations expanded their activities. In the late nineteenth century, social service agencies emerged as a concern of a small group of well-to-do women. In the twentieth century, such services expanded to include thousands of middle-class and working-class women in such organizations as Boy Scouts, Girl Scouts, parent-teacher associations, nursery schools, and a variety of town improvement and social welfare agencies. These interests have been largely supported by women volunteers.

The extension of interest in voluntary organizations at the turn of the century may be regarded as the forerunner of today's growing participation in paid employment. It helped to satisfy the dual need for companionship and creativity. The increase in participation in community affairs first occurred among the upper and middle income groups who were able to profit most from labor-saving devices for the home and who were best able to avail themselves of broadened educational opportunities. Moreover, we owe partly to the work performed in voluntary organizations during the first half of the twentieth century the growing acceptance of women's ability to work with men in non-domestic enterprises as they had formerly worked with them in wresting a subsistence from the soil.

In addition to these developments associated with the progress of the industrial revolution, other events and trends have played an important role in changing the concept of women's nature and abilities. The first of these in point of time was the settlement of the American frontier. The romanticized upper-class image of the wife as a delicate, dependent creature in need of protection began to fade as another image emerged — that of the woman capable of sharing with her husband the rigors and dangers of pioneer homesteading. Not only did the pioneer wife work beside her husband in providing food and shelter under most trying conditions, but she proved she could shoulder a rifle if need be. Though her husband undertook the heaviest tasks, she was no longer the sheltered wife but a companion and helpmate.

In the twentieth century, two world wars created manpower shortages, which greatly improved women's economic opportunities and contributed to an altered understanding of women's abilities and usefulness. Outside of nursing, women's work during World War I was done mostly through voluntary organizations, but World War II brought great expansion in other kinds of participation. Women helped fill the demand in such jobs as personnel management, supply and finance, transportation, communications and intelligence, as well as in other technical fields. Severe depressions in the years between the two world wars partially wiped out these gains because of sentiment against married women holding jobs needed by men. But with comparatively steadier employment opportunities since World War II, women's gains have been better consolidated, and prejudice against women holding jobs in competition with men has become somewhat less prevalent. In the last post-war era, larger business organizations, expanded activities of commerce and communication, and new systems of distribution and advertising have required the use of new resources of labor and thus have helped to change traditional attitudes concerning women's status in the labor force.

Although these specific events in our history have hastened progress in women's status and opportunities, American social and political idealism founded upon the belief in equality of opportunity has been of fundamental importance in creating a fuller life for women in this country. The results we have here discussed could not have been obtained if it had not been for the broadening of educational opportunities which have given women the chance for self-development. It was the democratic principle for which the feminists of the nineteenth century labored when they campaigned for equal rights. The leaders of this movement were mostly well-to-do and well-educated women, whose demands for civil and political equality stimulated the action to obtain equal educational opportunities with men — the chance for women also to live the good life of wider participation, ideas, and constructive leadership.

The women's colleges founded in the latter part of the nineteenth century rigorously undertook to dispel the concept quite generally held among the socially elite on the eastern seaboard — that the female of the species was a creature of delicate constitution and inferior mind, adapted physically, mentally, and temperamentally only for creating a home and rearing children. Professor Newcomer writes:

> One of Vassar's three original buildings was a gymnasium containing rooms for a riding school, calisthenics, and a bowling alley. The Main Building was provided with spacious corridors . . . to provide 'room for exercise in inclement weather.' And walks and drives 'full three miles in extent' were laid out on the campus to tempt the students outdoors when the weather favored.[3]

Perhaps the belief that women are inferior mentally was even more difficult to shake than that of their physical inadequacy. In the early

[3] Mabel Newcomer, *A Century of Higher Education for American Women* (New York: Harper & Bros., 1959), p. 28.

twentieth century, President Eliot of Harvard, speaking from that citadel of male learning, joined others of his generation in voicing disbelief in the intellectual equality of women with men. He said:

> The male and female minds are not alike. Sex penetrates the mind and the affections [of women], and penetrates deeply and powerfully. . . . Women differ from men more than men differ from each other; that is to say, there is a fundamental pervading difference between all men and all women which extends to their minds quite as much as to their bodies.[4]

Among the leading educators who disagreed with President Eliot was a no less eminent psychologist than President Angell of the University of Michigan, who said:

> I think I may fairly speak, from my years of experience, during which I have taught many thousands of women, . . . that there is little difference between my students, except that I generally have to attract the males a little more violently to have them attain the requirements. But I think I may say for sheer brilliancy many of the women under my charge have proved themselves superior to many of the men I have met and certainly taught.[5]

Now that women have, through higher education, demonstrated their mental ability, we still recognize possible differences in aptitudes for certain occupations. We are told that there are jobs for which, by and large, women seem to have an aptitude equal to that of men, some for which they have more and some less. In many instances, however, even the seeming discrepancies in aptitudes between men and women in certain fields are believed by psychologists to be caused as much by lingering social concepts concerning areas of work suitable for women as by inaptitude. We have assumed that certain fields are fit and others unfit for women. For many generations the belief in extreme differences between masculine and feminine abilities has persisted so strongly that from early childhood boys and girls have been reared according to patterns thought socially acceptable for each sex. The result has been that girls have been forced into a much narrower groove of participation than boys. Accordingly, they have been not only hampered in experience but psychologically prepared from early childhood for only the limited range of activities considered char-

---

[4] Thomas Woody, *History of Women's Education in the United States* (New York: Macmillan Co., 1904), II, 88–89.
[5] *Ibid.*, p. 91.

acteristically feminine. Today, however, as Professor Mabel Newcomer comments, "It is taken for granted today that women have a right to go all the way through to the doctor's degree in any field. That women are physically and mentally capable of being educated like men is an accepted fact."[6]

Again, the operation of the democratic principle in our American society has made women's employment socially acceptable by erasing the stigma associated with work in the minds of the upper and middle socio-economic classes. As Professor Smuts has pointed out in his study of women's work in this country, there have been certain developments which have "tended to eliminate sharp differences in American society. . . . The vast gulf between the rich and the poor has been narrowed."[7] Because of our laws curtailing immigration and of the assimilation of the second and third generations of the foreign-born, the labor demand which immigrants once supplied is now being met by the influx of the native-born from farms to city industries. Also, because wages of manual laborers have greatly increased, status distinctions are less sharp among various occupations. Particularly significant is the effect of free education upon the cultural and occupational training of the lower income workers, a factor which has greatly reduced the relative economic advantages of the wealthy and socially elite. Workmen's compensation, health and employment insurance, and pensions have also had a democratizing influence. Because of the greater economic security such measures have afforded, fewer women are now compelled to work on account of poverty. Correspondingly, women from the more well-to-do classes no longer hesitate to work because of a fear that their accepting paid employment will be interpreted as stemming from financial need.

These steady and long-run trends in changing conditions and social attitudes, and the resultant developments in the life patterns of women, are the important factors making possible present forecasts for women's employment, which we shall discuss in the next chapter.

[6] Newcomer, *op. cit.*, p. 2.
[7] Smuts, *op. cit.*, pp. 66–67.

CHAPTER 4

The Employed Woman: Facts and Forecasts

*Our conscience has been reawakened to the contribution
individuals can make not merely by being good parents but
also by using their individual gifts.*

MARGARET MEAD*

Of particular interest to young women today in planning their
futures is the comparatively recent appearance on the employment
scene of middle-class wives, few of whom worked before World War II.
Their numbers are rapidly increasing. In 1940, only 30 per cent of all
women workers were married; in March 1964, the figure was 57 per
cent.[1] In fact, the middle-class working wife is making an impressive
impact upon various facets of American life — economic, political,
sociological, and psychological.

The President's Commission on the Status of Women estimates that
a twenty-year-old girl, if she remains single, will spend some forty
years in the labor force. If, after working for a few years, she marries
and has a family, and then goes back to work in the labor force at
thirty, perhaps only part-time at first, she is likely to work for an average of twenty-three years more.

These facts show convincingly that in modern society every young
woman needs occupational training. The United States Department
of Labor estimates that eight or nine out of ten girls today will be
gainfully employed at some time during their lives. In contrast to past
decades, this pattern applies to young women of all income levels.

* Margaret Mead, Epilogue to *American Women*. The Report of the President's
Commission on the Status of Women (New York: Charles Scribner's Sons, 1965),
p. 202.

[1] *1965 Handbook on Women Workers* (U.S. Women's Bureau Bulletin No. 290
[Washington, D.C., 1966]), p. 19.

While at the turn of the century the majority of gainfully employed women were in the low-educational levels, in 1964–65 less than one-third of our workers had completed only grade-school training. In the same year, almost three-fifths of women college graduates were workers.[2]

Because of this trend and the prospect for further increase in demand for women workers in the near future, emphasis on occupational training for women will grow. Since 1940 American women have been responsible for the largest share in the growth of our labor force, accounting for 60 per cent of the total increase from 1940 to 1964. Today, they are more than one-third of all workers, and almost three out of five working women are married. Furthermore, it is estimated that the number of women workers will probably show a rise of 41 per cent between 1964 and 1980, compared with only 27 per cent for men.[3]

It is, of course, the large-scale entrance of married women into paid employment that has reactivated the discussion about women's roles. We shall talk about some of the effects of this development upon the working woman and her family in a later chapter. Here we are concerned only with the fact that middle-class wives are working in ever-increasing numbers, with understanding the reasons for this phenomenon, and with knowing which fields offer the most promising opportunities for college girls' future employment.

During the past decade the combined number of professional, office, and sales workers exceeded for the first time in our history the number of persons employed in manual occupations — skilled, semi-skilled, and unskilled jobs. As the machine replaces human labor, we have need for higher-class workers in higher-class jobs. This means more work opportunities for college-trained women. The U.S. Department of Labor predicts that during this decade and the one which follows this trend will continue, the fastest growth occurring in professional and technical occupations.[4] Today, as more women become better educated, many more of them are qualified for the higher-level work which is increasingly available.

For most married women the time during their lives when they work

[2] *Fact Sheet on Changing Patterns of Women's Lives* (U.S. Women's Bureau, Washington, D.C.), February, 1966.

[3] U.S. Women's Bureau, *1965 Handbook*, pp. 2–3, 221.

[4] *Manpower Challenge of the 1960's* (U.S. Bureau of Labor Statistics [Washington, D.C., 1960]), p. 10.

is dependent upon whether there are young children in the family. White mothers with children under six years of age are only about half as likely to be working as those with school-age children. For non-white mothers, the rate of participation is considerably higher (Table 3).

Table 3. **Labor-Force Participation Rates of White and Nonwhite Mothers (Husband Present), by Ages of Children, March 1964**
(Mothers 14 years of age and over)

Ages of children	Mothers in the labor force		Nonwhite as per cent of all working mothers
	White	Nonwhite	
	Number		
Total	6,987,000	932,000	11.7
	Per cent		
Children 6 to 17 years only	41.9	57.7	9.4
Children under 6 years[1]	21.4	33.7	15.4
None under 3 years	25.0	44.6	13.8
Some under 3 years	19.3	29.3	16.5

Source: U.S. Department of Labor, Bureau of Labor Statistics, Special Labor Force Report No. 50.

[1] May have some older children, in addition to one or more under 6.

The usual pattern which most women in this country are following today is a short period in paid employment immediately following marriage, then re-entry into the labor force when their children are older or are grown and leave home. Part-time work (less than thirty-five hours a week) or work for part of the year, or both, is the pattern for most employed mothers in families where the children are very young. Those who work full time are most likely to work for only part of the year, often in seasonal occupations.[5]

The personal motives which women attribute to working outside the home are varied. The majority of working wives in the low-income and the lower range of the middle-income brackets are supplementing inadequate family income, helping to raise the family's standard of living, or pay for a home or their children's education.[6] Among the better educated, there are often one or more additional reasons for

[5] U.S. Women's Bureau, *1965 Handbook*, pp. 36–37, 43–44.
[6] *Ibid.*, p. 5.

working — to use more fully their abilities and training, to spend leisure in an interesting pursuit, to be of greater social usefulness, and to receive social recognition for their attainments.

Figures compiled by the U.S. Women's Bureau show us the differences in median income between the families in which the wife works and those in which she does not. In 1964, out of the 41.6 million husband-wife families in this country, 13.6 million of them had both husband and wife working. The median income for the total 41.6 million families was $6,932. For the 13.6 million in which the husband and wife both worked the median income was $8,170; where the wife did not work, the figure was $6,338. Sixty-two per cent of the families with working wives received $7,000 or more annually, as compared with only 43 per cent in families where the wife did not work.[7]

The wife's decision about whether, when, and how much to work, and the manner in which the money she earns is spent, all depend on a number of factors. These differ with financial need, the particular stage of the family cycle, the customary standard of living and of values in the couple's past experience, and the level of their ambitions and social expectations. But, allowing for these wide variations, there exist certain universal characteristics in the economic goals and attempts to satisfy them at the several different stages of the family life cycle. The following summary of these differentiations is taken from a study made by Professor Frances Feldman of the School of Social Work of the University of Southern California.[8]

With young couples, the wife's earnings fit into one of three general patterns. One couple may plan to live on the husband's earnings and save the wife's for major extra expenses — having a baby or buying a house and furniture — although the actual house purchase is usually not initiated until the husband is about twenty-five years old. Another couple may spend the wife's additional earnings for comforts and luxuries they might not otherwise be able to buy until later years. Automobile and television ownership have first priorities in most cases. Still another may, because of poor management or the husband's low income, find themselves in debt, in which case the wife seeks employment to reduce the couple's indebtedness.

[7] *Ibid.*, p. 125.

[8] Frances Lomas Feldman, "Supplementary Income Earned by Married Women," in *Work in the Lives of Married Women* (National Manpower Council Publication [New York: Columbia University Press, 1958]), pp. 94–106.

When the wife withdraws from paid employment because of pregnancy and increased home responsibilities, the family experiences simultaneously a current loss of income and mounting expenses. This is the stage in the family life cycle when financial strain is most likely to be felt. It is the period in which the young couple who have been able to save a substantial part of the wife's income will appreciate the financial cushion which her recent earnings can provide. Professor Feldman points out that the family usually reaches its maximum size when the father is around thirty, its maximum income when the father is over forty-five. Therefore, before the period of peak income, the family is faced with increased costs of medical care, added household equipment to ease the work for the growing family, extra opportunities for the children, and installment payments for a house. In other words, there are more fixed payments to meet at this time than at any other. This fact no doubt figures largely in some wives' returning to work at a time when they are also most needed at home. Having once returned to work, they will very likely remain there until their children's education is completed.

The number of wives entering the labor force increases at the next stage in the family life cycle when the children are grown. At this point, the motive is less likely to be necessity than procuring extra comforts and luxuries the couple could not have in abundance, if at all, during the period of the growing family. With the husband now receiving his maximum salary, no children to support, and the house and its durable equipment paid for, there is more freedom of choice in how to spend the extra income earned by the wife. The following table, published by the U.S. Women's Bureau, shows the rapid and steady increase since 1940 in the per cent of employed women at all ages after thirty-five (Table 4. See also Chart I).

What are the net gains of employment to the married woman? The extra costs incurred frequently result in a smaller net financial gain than the couple had anticipated. Often they have not realized the amounts the wife will need for transportation, lunches and coffee-breaks, more and better clothes, and perhaps extra for household help and commercial laundry services, not to mention the substantial increase in the amount of their income tax. However, in such estimates intangible benefits must be counted, such as improved morale of the wife because she has more money to spend, can afford better grooming, and can perhaps rid herself of some of the drudgery of housework.

Table 4. **Trend in Labor-Force Participation of Women, By Age**

Age	Women workers as per cent of women population			
	1965	*1960*	*1950*	*1940*
Total	37.3	36.3	32.1	27.6
14 to 17 years	15.7	16.6	16.8	8.2
18 to 24 years	47.7	46.2	44.8	46.4
25 to 34 years	38.2	35.9	33.6	35.5
35 to 44 years	46.8	44.3	38.2	29.4
45 to 54 years	50.3	49.5	37.1	24.5
55 to 64 years	41.4	37.4	27.6	18.0
65 years and over	10.5	10.8	9.7	6.9

Source: U.S. Department of Labor, Bureau of Labor Statistics: Employment and Earnings, May 1965, and Special Labor Force Report No. 14. U.S. Department of Commerce, Bureau of the Census: Current Population Reports, P-57, No. 94, and P-50, Nos. 22 and 32.

She may also feel that having a paid job improves her personal status.

One certain effect of the supplementary income earned by such a large percentage of wives is the rise in the average family income and of the proportion of families in the middle-income bracket. In general, their employment usually makes possible a better standard of living and pays for additional advantages for the children. In our next chapter, we must balance against these economic gains some of the possible sociological and psychological effects that should be weighed by families in which the wife works.

Can the young woman who plans farther ahead than merely for her immediate future depend upon present forecasts of great variety in job opportunities? What are some of the occupations other than the few most usual ones which women are now entering? Are there some opportunities of which most women seem to be unaware?

The next decade, as well as this one, will probably bring especially wide opportunities in women's employment because this country will need all of its workers who have marketable skills and talents. With the continued growth of the economy, a factor which will favor an unusual demand for women workers is the change in the age distribution of our population. We will have proportionately small numbers in the preferred working age of twenty-six to forty-four years to support the large numbers in the two extremes of the age scale. In other words, the middle-aged segment in the population will have increased only 5 per cent between 1958 and 1970, while those under twenty-five years of age will have increased 45 per cent, and older ages 23 per cent (Chart III). This situation has been created by the accelerated birth rate in the years following World War II and longer life spans resulting from medical and environmental factors.

Women's greatest gains are characteristically made during times of such labor shortage. Two world wars, especially World War II, opened opportunities in women's employment that had hitherto been little known. With the continuance of the present rate of economic growth, the prospects are that this decade and the next will continue to be another of these periods of greatly expanded demand for trained workers on a scale which will necessitate developing new sources of labor supply. The downward employment trend of those over sixty-five is expected to continue; and it is anticipated that the percentage of school and college enrollments will continue to climb, reducing the potential number of young workers. Early marriages and high birth rates will probably still further restrict the availability of young women. Obviously, this situation points to interesting possibilities in expanding employment opportunities for women. The U.S. Department of Labor's 1960 prediction of six million more women workers in 1970 than in 1960 represents a 25 per cent increase for women compared with only 15 per cent for men.[9]

That the current sharp rise in women's employment rate is not an isolated phenomenon peculiar to this and the next decade provides further assurance that favorable economic opportunities for women will continue to increase. In 1965, there were 10 per cent more of the total women's population working than in 1940, 15 per cent more than in 1920, and 17 per cent more than in 1900. Moreover, in contrast to the present picture, women workers at the turn of the century came mostly from the lower income levels.[10]

But there are qualifications of this optimistic forecast. With the demand for trained workers increasing and with greater numbers now receiving college education, competition for the best jobs will become keener. Furthermore, in this period of growing automation, with much routine work being done by machines, the opportunities are multi-

[9] U.S. Bureau of Labor Statistics, *op. cit.*, p. 7.
[10] U.S. Women's Bureau, *1965 Handbook*, p. 6.

Chart III

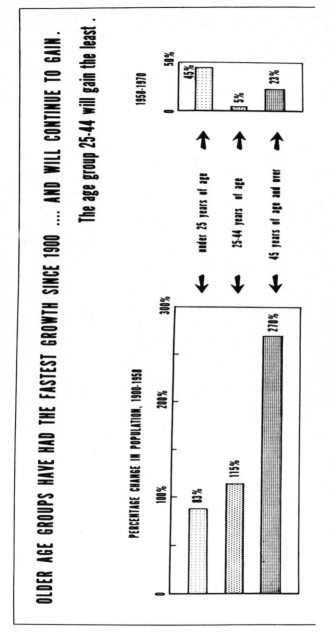

OLDER AGE GROUPS HAVE HAD THE FASTEST GROWTH SINCE 1900 .... AND WILL CONTINUE TO GAIN.

The age group 25-44 will gain the least.

PERCENTAGE CHANGE IN POPULATION, 1900-1958

under 25 years of age

25-44 years of age

45 years of age and over

1958-1970

Source: U.S. Department of Labor, *Employing Older Workers.*

plying most rapidly in positions requiring both education and training. The changing character of work in clerical occupations illustrates this point. The number of jobs in this field increased from 2½ million in 1940 to almost 8 million in 1965, a growth directly related to expanded activities of business corporations, large-scale financial organizations, mail order and other retail establishments, government operations, and many other types of undertakings. But, because of recent inventions relating to office machines which have mechanized office processes to a greatly increased extent, better-trained clerical workers with special technical and mechanical abilities are needed, rather than general clerical workers able to perform only fairly simple and routine tasks.[11]

College women are now found primarily in the professions, and today they have a wide variety from which to choose. It is true that most women are in fields which are traditionally feminine, for custom and social attitudes continue to work to a considerable degree against the use of other special aptitudes or encouragement of other inclinations girls may have. Unfortunately, some departments in our universities as well as too many school advisors often follow convention in discouraging girls who are tempted to enter traditionally masculine professions. And the girl who follows an accepted feminine line is still more likely to be quickly placed in a job, except in those traditionally masculine professions with especially keen demand. However, such a demand now exists in a number of masculine fields, and a break with this tradition is occurring.

The U.S. Women's Bureau points out that during the 1950's, the fields in which women made their most outstanding employment gains — either in terms of percentage increase or numbers of workers — were those relating to the service and social needs of our population. Listed among the professions in which the number of women more than doubled during this period were:

mathematicians
personnel and labor relations workers
public relations workers and publicity writers
recreation and group workers
sports instructors and officials

11 *Ibid.*, pp. 96–97.

In other professional occupations the number of women increased from 30 to 60 per cent, such as:

accountants and auditors	musicians and music teachers
college presidents, professors and instructors	nurses
	physicians and surgeons
editors and reporters	teachers
librarians	therapists and healers

Among the jobs in which women made numerically small but noteworthy gains (10 to 30 per cent) were:

dietitians and nutritionists	religious workers
engineers	social scientists
lawyers and judges	social, welfare, and
natural scientists	recreation workers

The Bureau comments in summary that, "It is apparent that job horizons will continue to widen for the college woman in the 1960's. Challenging careers for qualified college women have never before existed in such variety — nor offered so many rewards."[12]

Teaching, which has always been the principal occupation of college-trained women, is declining somewhat in relative popularity, as other professions open to them. Even so, according to the U.S. Bureau of Labor Statistics, in April 1965 the number of women teachers (except college) at work equaled 42 per cent of all professional women.[13] Although girls with only a high school diploma are those usually found in office jobs, some college graduates have preferred this occupation to teaching because work conditions are good, hours are short, and they work in association with men.

In summary, we may say that women are now entering professions never dreamed of at the opening of the century. Since 1930 their participation in the traditionally women's professions — social work, teaching, library work, and nursing — has shown a decline, and their entry into several of the traditionally men's professions has been on the rise. The inference we seem justified in drawing is that we are beginning to see a breaking down of strict segregation between professions that have been regarded as either exclusively masculine or

---

[12] *Job Horizons for College Women in the 1960's* (U.S. Women's Bureau Publication No. 288 [Washington, D.C., 1964]), p. 71.

[13] U.S. Women's Bureau, *1965 Handbook*, p. 93.

exclusively feminine, giving women today a much wider choice (Table 5).

It will be helpful for any young woman looking forward to professional preparation to make use of publications she can obtain from the Women's Bureau of the U.S. Department of Labor at very nominal cost. One illustration of such material is its 1960 bulletin, *Job Horizons for College Women in the 1960's,* which briefly describes thirty-two professions and gives the addresses of a number of headquarters of professional organizations where more detailed information may be requested. The editors point out that because the full range of professional occupations open to college women is very extensive, the pamphlet includes only some of the largest and most promising fields.

The Women's Bureau, in collaboration with the National Vocational Guidance Association, voices concern that there are a great many professional opportunities of which women do not seem to be aware, or at least of which they are not fully availing themselves. They further suggest that in professions with equally as strong need as that in teaching and nursing women seem to have insufficient motivation to receive suitable training, and that "to attract more women into these fields, a greater awareness may be needed not only on the part of young women, but by parents and counselors that employment opportunities are expanding rapidly in these professions and that women who have entered them have not only demonstrated their competence but are gaining recognition."[14] Among the fields which they specify are the physical sciences, the biological sciences, the social sciences, mathematics, and engineering.

A number of agencies have been making efforts for several years to recruit women in certain fields. In 1962 the *Wall Street Journal* published the results of a survey it had made of thirty college placement officials and fifty corporation personnel executives. It found that many companies were after all the women they could sign up as scientists, technicians, and mathematicians, and that the supply was frequently so limited that recruiting efforts were insufficient to supply their demands. More women were found to be going into market research and investments, also a field in which there is too limited a supply of applicants. Insurance seems to be an area of widening opportunities.

[14] *First Jobs for College Women* (U.S. Women's Bureau Publications No. 168 [Washington, D.C., 1959]), p. 15.

Table 5. Women in Professional, Technical, and Kindred Occupations, 1960 and 1950

Occupation	1960		1950		Per cent increase 1950-1960
	Number	Per cent	Number	Per cent	
Total employed	2,753,052	100.0	1,951,072	100.0	41
Teachers[1]	1,196,526	43.5	839,229	43.0	43
Nurses, professional	567,884	20.6	390,594	20.0	45
Musicians, music teachers ..	109,638	4.0	78,111	4.0	40
Accountants, auditors	79,045	2.9	56,011	2.9	41
Librarians	71,836	2.6	49,267	2.5	46
Social, welfare, recreation workers	60,667	2.2	52,527	2.7	15
College presidents, professors, instructors	38,850	1.4	29,991	1.5	30
Editors, reporters	37,438	1.4	26,758	1.4	40
Religious workers	35,099	1.3	29,037	1.5	21
Personnel, labor relations workers	30,215	1.1	15,093	.8	100
Sports instructors, officials ..	24,931	.9	11,183	.6	123
Dietitians, nutritionists	24,237	.9	21,132	1.1	15
Therapists, healers	19,752	.7	12,176	.6	62
Physicians, surgeons	15,573	.6	11,752	.6	32
Recreation group workers ..	15,497	.6	6,763	.3	129
Natural scientists	14,738	.5	13,354	.7	10
Social scientists	14,177	.5	11,412	.6	24
Lawyers, judges	7,434	.3	6,271	.3	19
Engineers, technical	7,211	.3	6,499	.3	11
Pharmacists	7,129	.3	7,295	.4[2]	2
Public relations workers, publicity writers	7,005	.3	1,958	.1	258
Other occupations	368,230	13.4	274,659	14.1	37

Source: U. S. Department of Commerce, Bureau of the Census: 1960 Census of Population.

[1] Category does not include art, music, dancing, or physical education teachers.

[2] A decrease instead of an increase.

The Metropolitan Life Insurance Company now admits women to its middle management training program and trains girls with backgrounds in mathematics to be actuaries, determining insurance rates on the basis of life expectancies and other factors. The *Wall Street Journal* also noted that in Chicago, a prominent insurance company planned to hire twenty-five to thirty-five women college graduates in 1962, compared with five a year before. This survey also found retailing, a field long open to women, to be an occupation providing them a large number of jobs. It quoted Abraham & Straus of New York as saying that retailing is one of the best bets for a girl looking for a job. The demand for women merchandising trainees was reported to have doubled in three years as a result of the growth of shopping centers and branch stores.[15]

In choosing a field of specialization a young woman should be guided not only by what she thinks she would like to do immediately after graduation from college. For, if she marries, these first years of paid work may be her shortest. She should try to anticipate her probable return to the labor market after her children are grown. Of course, the question which immediately arises is how she can anticipate her later choice of occupation; her interest in the field of her original selection may continue or it may change. Furthermore, jobs for which workers are trained now may change in character in years to come. Speaking to this point, Jean A. Wells, Acting Chief of the Division of Research and Manpower Development Program, U.S. Department of Labor, advises that, "we must, therefore, seek job versatility by attaining related skills which can be used to obtain related employment. The slogan 'education for contingency' is becoming increasingly pertinent. It implies preparing for several alternative possibilities relating to a primary skill in order to meet a variety of contingencies. It is axiomatic, therefore, that continuing education and training are the order of the day."[16] We shall think about this program of job training during the later years in another chapter.

Whatever a young woman anticipates her own inclinations will be about returning to paid employment at a later period in her life, this pattern promises to be the choice for the majority of American

15 *Wall Street Journal* (Chicago Edition), February 1, 1962, p. 1.
16 Jean A. Wells, "Women and Girls in the Labor Market Today and Tomorrow," Address at the Annual Forum of the National Conference on Social Welfare, Cleveland, Ohio (U.S. Women's Bureau, Washington, D.C., 1963).

women, and their participation in the labor market is becoming a valuable national asset. This situation would seem to provide a fortunate coordination between the personal needs of older women to find added purpose and usefulness and our growing economy's need for trained manpower.

An impressive fact is the steady rise in the employment rate for women forty-five years old and over. A considerable portion of our managerial and skilled workers are now in the older age brackets, and they are reported to have the ability and work experience needed by our economy. The labor force participation of women forty-five to fifty-four years of age has risen from 24 per cent of the total women population in 1940 to 51 per cent in 1964, and the number is expected to be 59 per cent by 1980.[17] (Tables 1, 4). The median age of women workers has risen from twenty-six years in 1900 to forty-one years in 1965.

The U.S. Department of Labor and other agencies have made suggestions for speeding this trend of employment of women and older workers by encouraging still better adjustment of work schedules in accordance with physical ability and time available to such employees. It is probable that in the near future there will be a substantial increase in part-time work, a circumstance which will greatly facilitate participation in paid employment for older women who have lessened home responsibilities, as well as for young wives. The use of part-time workers appears to be a growing necessity if labor management is to avail itself of the contributions of our total trained manpower potential.[18]

In 1965, the President's Commission on the Status of Women reported that of the one in three married women who are working (almost one in two for non-whites), nearly a third work part-time, and three-fifths of all part-time work is done by married women.[19] The Commission points out that "inflexibility with regard to part-time employment in most current hiring systems, alike in government and in private enterprise, excludes the use of much able and available trained womanpower."[20]

[17] U.S. Women's Bureau, *1965 Handbook*, p. 222.
[18] U.S. Bureau of Labor Statistics, *op. cit.*, p. 18.
[19] *American Women*. The Report of the President's Commission on the Status of Women (New York: Charles Scribner's Sons), p. 45.
[20] *Ibid.*, p. 21.

Some students of labor problems see in the more extensive employment of married women under the conditions we have discussed a contribution to a healthier employment situation, due to the fact that women constitute a relatively flexible labor supply. A sizable proportion of the married women are secondary family wage earners, who work not so much from great necessity as from desire for supplementary income. Whenever the expected demand for additional manpower for our growing economy is interrupted by brief recessions, married women, who usually have less job seniority, will in many instances be among the first lay-offs. For most of them the temporary loss of a job brings less hardship to their families than the lay-off of the primary breadwinner. Likewise, the employer will benefit by usually being able to employ them again when times are good.[21] Obviously, the fact that they occupy a vulnerable position as part of the labor supply is not a satisfactory situation for women of equal training and ability with men. But until cyclical fluctuations in economic activity can be better controlled, periods of peak employment offer women opportunities which bring their abilities one step nearer to public recognition.

Amid the conditions which point to greatly expanded occupational opportunities for women, the importance of education can not be too strongly emphasized. We shall look at broader aspects of this topic in later chapters. Here, it is important to note how the degree of educational attainment by women has affected their job status. In 1962 almost 75 per cent of the employed women with 4 years or more of college held professional jobs. Almost 15 per cent held clerical jobs and approximately 5 per cent were managers and officials. On the other hand, of the employed women who had 1 to 3 years of college, only 28 per cent held professional jobs, and of those with only a high school diploma a mere 6 per cent were in professional occupations.[22] The upward trend in white-collar jobs — professional, office, and sales — which we have recently experienced is expected to continue. The U.S. Department of Labor forecasts the fastest growth among professional and technical occupations requiring education and training.

The degree of educational attainment largely determines the aver-

[21] H. S. Kaltenborn, "Utilizing Older Women Workers," in *Work in the Lives of Married Women,* p. 61.

[22] U.S. Women's Bureau, *Job Horizons,* p. 70.

age income for both men and women. From the following chart it will be observed that in 1964 the full-time median income of women with five or more years of college was $5,518. This was nearly $1600 above the median income of those who were college graduates only, and about $3000 more than those with only one to three years of college[23] (Chart IV).

However, in spite of this favorable relationship between job status and education, women's earnings are usually lower than men's. This situation results largely from differences in the types and levels of jobs women hold and in amount of their education and training. Women hold relatively few of the top-level administrative positions, and they have often been paid at lower rates than men even though they do the same kind of work. A federal law became effective June 11, 1964 providing that every employer having employees subject to the act must pay equal rates within an establishment to men and women doing equal work on jobs requiring equal skill, effort, and responsibility which are performed under similar working conditions. As of October 1965, twenty-five states had also passed equal pay laws.

Problems of preferences between men and women in professional advancement do not lend themselves so easily to legislative regulation. The late President Kennedy's Commission on the Status of Women found that:

> While the advancement rate for men and women differs considerably according to occupation, the overall difference in median grade in white-collar occupations is about five grades. Some three-quarters of the men are in grades reached by one quarter of the women. Differences are less sharp in such highly professional groups as attorneys, but in most cases women with comparable education and years of service are at lower grades than men. The women in the higher grades are somewhat older than the men; more of them have college degrees. Typically, they are married; those who are have smaller families than men in the same grade. The advancement of single women is noticeably but not strikingly greater than that of married women.[24]

Although prejudice against women in many types of employment is still a handicap to their receiving higher positions and pay, in many

---

[23] U.S. Women's Bureau, *1965 Handbook,* p. 133.
[24] *American Women, op. cit.,* p. 33.

Chart IV. Education and Earning Power Go Together

(MEDIAN INCOME IN 1964 OF WOMEN, BY YEARS OF SCHOOL COMPLETED, 1965)

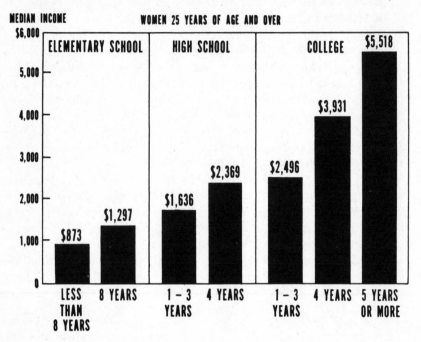

Source: *1965 Handbook on Women Workers,* U.S. Women's Bureau Bulletin 290, based on data from the Department of Commerce, Bureau of the Census.

instances it is not easy to determine whether this factor alone is responsible for their lack of equal recognition and advancement. One among several reasons for differentials in pay and in job status is the fact that women lose in job seniority and work experience between the time they leave the labor force to marry and rear a family and the time they return to work. Knowledge of this fact contributes to the reluctance of many employers to give them equal opportunities for advancement. However, an important factor in the acceleration of gains in women's status during the past few decades is their wider education and training. If the forecast concerning women's greater paid employment opportunities in the near future proves to be realistic, the degree to which young women avail themselves of higher education will largely determine their share in gainful employment.

CHAPTER 5

A Woman's Right to Choose

True equality can only mean the right to be uniquely creative.

ERIK H. ERIKSON*

Today, an essential part of every young woman's education consists in cultivating an awareness of the expanding range of alternatives in feminine life patterns which will enable her to harmonize her function as wife and mother with a fuller realization of herself as an individual.

Perhaps the most important by-product of the late nineteenth century feminist movement was the establishment, although somewhat limited in immediate application, of the right of choice for women whose life pattern was not dictated by economic necessity. During the century in which this principle has become more widely recognized, reactions to it have been eratic and extreme. The feminists often exercised the right of choice by renouncing marriage to pursue a career. In two world wars, especially in the second one, American women in great numbers enthusiastically responded to the need for increased manpower by entering practically all the occupations which had hitherto been traditionally regarded as masculine. Then, after having broken down much prejudice against their employment and, in many instances, having the way opened to continue in paid work, they decided against careers and well-paying jobs. Instead, in overwhelmingly large numbers, they chose marriage, and, if possible, a home in the suburbs. They elected this choice by relinquishing a college education entirely or by leaving college before the course was

* Erik H. Erikson, "Reflections on Womanhood" in *Daedalus*. The Journal of the American Academy of Arts and Sciences. XCIII, No. 2 (Spring 1964), p. 605.

completed. The records from the end of World War II to 1960 show a sharp decline both in academic achievement and in professional attainment.[1] Young women then welcomed all that complete domesticity implies — the rounds of household chores, a life of rapid childbearing — and they glamorized the whole process by developing the cult of the "feminine mystique."

Margaret Mead points out that this "tremendous swing back into the home is still in force," but that within the past five years there has been "some rebellion, chiefly engineered by women who are no longer fully engrossed with the care of young children."[2] But considering the implications of the post-war surge of women returning to domestic life, it appears that in advising women on life planning, we cannot ignore the strength of these elemental urges in the feminine nature.

It then would seem that one of the most hopeful aspects of the progress toward women's social adjustment is a recognition of the widening variety of choice in feminine life patterns. In contrast to the single alternative of marriage *or* career in the feminist era, our choice can be marriage or career, or *both*. The single most important condition favoring this enlargement of choice is the extension in the length of the average life span, which gives women time for both marriage and family *and* a paying job or, better yet, a career.

Another development furthering women's opportunities for choice is our national awakening within the past decade to our present waste in human resources. We have caught a vision of a modern Utopia in which the discovery, development, and better use of each individual's innate abilities could effect vast improvements in the human condition. Accordingly, we have become suddenly more conscious of the great waste of talent and ability among women. We are nearer to being ready to ask if the greatest fulfillment of *every* woman's capabilities is in devoting her life to nurturing children. Perhaps some especially talented women do not enjoy such a role and can best contribute to human welfare by developing their superior aptitudes for the professions. Because of the almost universal preference among women for

---

[1] John B. Parrish, "Professional Womanpower as a National Resource," *Quarterly Review of Economics and Business,* Vol. I, No. 1 (University of Illinois, February, 1961), pp. 54–63.

[2] Margaret Mead, Epilogue in *American Women.* The President's Report on the Status of Women. (New York: Charles Scribner's Sons, 1965), p. 194.

marriage and family, those who make the choice of career will be in the minority but, because we need to search out and develop all talent, and because choice should be the right of every woman, we must recognize and honor the election of this alternative. Furthermore, in the face of our problems of overpopulation, no woman need now regard procreation as one of her bounden duties.

But for those who have the almost universal preference for marriage and a family, there are several important choices to be made in life planning, for we can predict from reliable studies of present statistics that in addition to having a family they will spend an average of twenty-five years in paid employment. Only a decade ago, the forecast of these impending decisions would probably have seemed unrealistic to most young women. But today there is considerable evidence on college campuses that many girls are anticipating a period of paid employment after the early years of marriage and child-rearing, although there is still too much indifference to preparing for this future.

That such a prospect still seems so much outside the concern of many young women perhaps results largely from the fact that the sharp increase in the employment rate of married women is a relatively new development and is not as evident in the more rural communities. For those who do not clearly foresee the necessity for planning their lives, a most significant factor in this lack of awareness is their immediate intense involvement with marriage as their all-inclusive goal. Throughout the high school and college years and during the usual brief earning period afterwards, young women are affected so strongly by pressures for marriage and homemaking that more comprehensive planning for their futures, which is so much a part of the thought pattern of young men, is overlooked. Moreover, girls of this age have usually been given little opportunity to know that by middle years, and sometimes earlier, the modern educated woman feels the need for additional means of self-realization outside her home. She has time, energy, and skills that can be fully utilized only by her assuming a dual role.

An interesting illustration of the modern woman's desire for larger opportunities to use her full potential is found in the requests which come to the Vocational Bureau of Vassar College. Here, evidence mounts that there is little interest of girls in returning to professional work in the first five to ten years after graduation. But after that,

Vassar graduates request the help of the Bureau in securing jobs. And it is in a *job* that most of them in this age bracket are interested, not in a *career*.[3] This preference for a job in contrast to a career implies that these young women are interested in work that can be combined with their homemaking.

A survey recently conducted by the U.S. Women's Bureau in co-operation with the Alumnae Advisory Center in New York City provides testimony on the interest of college women in paid employment. Women who had been out of college for about fifteen years were surveyed on the assumption that many were at an age when they were thinking about changing their pattern of living. The information was obtained during the winter of 1960–61 from five hundred graduates and eighty non-graduates out of the six hundred and seventy-four alumnae (class of 1945) for four liberal arts colleges. The percentage of these alumnae already employed ranged in the several colleges from 16 to 45 per cent. Only 8 to 20 per cent reported no interest in future employment.[4]

In the present situation, where there exists the need of the mature woman for work and of our economy for workers, choices of whether or not to work are seldom complicated. The difficult choice which a young woman will face concerns the possibility of work some time during the child-rearing period. First, should she, or should she not, participate in gainful employment during this period? Second, if she does, at what time in her life cycle should she work?

Before discussing these points, it may be helpful to know some of the facts about the number of mothers now employed in relation to the ages of their children. If we examine the figures, we find that ages of children is a largely determining factor. More than one in three mothers without children under eighteen is in the labor force (36.5 per cent). For all mothers with children under eighteen the figure is nearly the same (35.0 per cent). But within the latter bracket there is a marked difference in percentages depending upon the ages of the children. Close to half of the mothers with children between six and seventeen are working (45.7 per cent), while only one in four of those with children under six is in the labor force (25.3 per cent).

[3] Claire Cox, "Vassar Girls Want Jobs, Not Careers," *Wall Street Journal*, August 6, 1961.

[4] *Fifteen Years After College — A Study of Alumnae, Class of 1945* (U.S. Women's Bureau Bulletin No. 283 [Washington, D.C., 1962]).

Within this last category, the percentage again varies by ages of children. Among those with children under six, but none under three, almost one in three is working (32.1 per cent), while only about one in five mothers with children under three is employed (21.4 per cent).[5] If we knew what proportion of these young mothers were working part-time and what proportion were working full-time, this factor could also show differences in percentages.

So much for the present. What are the future prospects? Because of the factors differentiating mothers from other employees, the percentage increase in their employment is difficult to predict, but we can assume a growth in their employment rate consistent with trends in the employment rate of all married women. The U.S. Department of Labor predicts that women workers will probably show a rise of 41 per cent between 1964 and 1980, compared with only 27 per cent for men. Of this growth, 87 per cent is accounted for by the expected increase in population and 13 per cent by the continued rise in the labor force participation rates of adult women. For a more exact understanding of these figures, it must be pointed out that, although there will undoubtedly be some increase in the percentage of employed mothers with children under eighteen, the Department of Labor expects the sharpest rise in the rate for women in the forty-five to fifty-four-year-old group with a somewhat smaller yet sizable increase for women fifty-five to fifty-nine years old.[6]

We must bear in mind that the foregoing facts relate to the percentages of employed women in *all* socio-economic classes, while our considerations here concern mostly those of the upper and middle classes whose economic status and educational background permit them choices. In any study of this nature, this distinction must not be overlooked. The contrasting statements made by the U.S. Department of Labor and by Nye and Hoffman in their study of employed women serve to illustrate this point. The government studies show that at least half of all women work out of economic necessity, and include women who are heads of families — widowed, divorced, or separated from their husbands, and those who have to help support their children — who have disabled husbands, or husbands in low-income occupations.[7]

[5] *Background Factors on Women Workers* (Women's Bureau, U.S. Department of Labor, May 1966), p. 11.

[6] *1965 Handbook on Women Workers* (Women's Bureau, U.S. Department of Labor Bulletin No. 290, 1965), p. 221.

[7] *Why Women Work.* Pamphlet. (Women's Bureau, U.S. Department of Labor, February 1966).

Obviously, few of these can choose whether or not to work. On the other hand, the Nye and Hoffman study is more interested in the trend of maternal employment in the middle-class family. Their findings point out that within this group during the last two decades a transition has been made "from a situation in which women were *forced* into employment, with their labor the primary source of family income, to one in which women are *drawn* into employment to raise family living standards and for other reasons.[8]

Another word of caution is also necessary in interpreting the meaning of economic necessity. A standard of living which may be adequate at one socio-economic level may be quite insufficient by the standards of persons in another social stratum. Also because economic necessity means different things to different individuals, the number of women actually working for this reason is difficult to determine. Unfortunately, some young mothers are motivated to work by neurotic sense of competition with families in the same or a higher income bracket. These women often rationalize their money-making activities by stating other reasons for their employment which they think will be more sure of having public approval. Where such social striving or mere boredom with child-rearing is the sole motivation, mothers of young children might ask themselves whether their efforts to satisfy their competitive strivings are as beneficial as the contribution they could make in satisfying the emotional requirements of their children and in giving them better guidance.

The reasons for married women entering paid employment which were enumerated in the previous chapter are today the most usual, and in mothers' decisions about whether or not to work, the maximum well-being of the entire family is usually taken into consideration. Undoubtedly the greatest good of the children is the first concern, but that of the husband and the wife herself must be recognized. Nye and Hoffman point out that our child-rearing philosophy is undergoing change from one which defers less to the child and expects more of a contribution from him. We are developing more of a "person-centered" rather than a "child-centered" family philosophy, recognizing the psychological needs of each member of the group.[9] This viewpoint results in our asking what is best for the child, what is best for the husband, and what is best for the mother herself.

[8] F. Ivan Nye and Lois Wladis Hoffman, *The Employed Woman in America* (Chicago: Rand McNally and Co., 1963), pp. 12, 13.
[9] *Ibid.*, p. 26.

Because the large-scale employment of married women is a recent phenomenon, only within the past decade have we become keenly aware of a need for answers to these questions through research. In the Preface to *Womanpower,* published by the National Manpower Council, meeting at Columbia University in 1957, Ambassador James D. Zeller, former chairman of the Council, declared that even though the outlines of the revolution in women's employment were by that time quite visible, all of its implications for American life were not understood. He added that it would be quite unrealistic to assume that the participation of so many wives and mothers in paid employment would not have "consequences for patterns of family life, the development of children during their formative years, or the greater sharing of homemaking functions by husband and wife."

The remarks at this conference with regard to the welfare of children by Katherine Oettinger, Chief of the Children's Bureau of the U.S. Department of Health, Education, and Welfare, are still applicable to efforts at research in this area:

> We at the Children's Bureau are often asked, these days, what are the effects on children of maternal employment? To that question we have a single answer, loud and clear: 'It depends.' It depends on the kind of mother, the kind of child, the kind of family. It depends, among other things, on why the mother works, how much she works, what she does, what her work does to and for her, how old her children are, what provision she makes for them while she works, how they perceive the fact of her working. . . . Each of these is loaded with further qualifications and all of them qualify each other. Subject to these complex and interlocking provisos, I can summarize one part of our position by saying that — other things being equal — we think that few mothers with children under six, and fewer mothers with children under three, are able to carry a full-time job and also fill the needs of their children in these crucial and vulnerable early years. But other things are not always equal. Therefore, the qualifications and the need to discuss them.[10]

In the midst of such inquiries as those which prompted Mrs. Oettinger's response, the Children's Bureau expressed itself as not having sufficient dependable research evidence concerning the effects

[10] Katherine B. Oettinger, "Maternal Employment and Children," in *Work in the Lives of Married Women* (National Manpower Council publication [New York: Columbia University Press, 1958]), pp. 133–139.

on families and children of maternal employment, *per se*. Subsequently, within the past few years, several competent research projects have been carried on in this area, and many more are needed. Because of the many facets of the subject which must be studied and the many variables to be considered in each area of the research, results are still largely inconclusive, but it will be of value to note some of the available findings.

We can begin our thinking with the certain premise that homemaking during the early family years is a full-time job, and that the skills required are probably quite as exacting as those necessary in many of the professions. We have already noted that improvements in household technology may not have brought about as much change in the amount of time spent by a woman as in the character of the tasks she performs. From this assumption, we must reason that in instances where the mother of young children undertakes employment outside the home, many of the tasks connected with child-care during her working hours must be done by a substitute.

How much do we know about the effects of substitute care upon the development of the child? Eleanor Maccoby of the Harvard Department of Social Relations points out that the formation of the child's behavior pattern and his emotional stability may be endangered if he is supervised by a large number of different persons.[11] Generally, during infancy and childhood he is more likely to prosper under his mother's care than that of a substitute. Even for an older child, a requirement of first importance is that responsibility for training him and controlling him in the mother's absence be given to one person.

We may assume that most mothers care enough for the welfare of their children to provide as good a substitute as possible during their absence. However, it is often impossible to find a substitute who is entirely satisfactory for the situation, for it is desirable to have someone who is not only responsible but whose attitudes are similar to the mother's. It is not always possible to be sure in advance what the attitude of such a person will be. Tendencies toward strictness and permissiveness are seldom the same in two individuals, and inconsistency in these matters may confuse the child and lead to poor habit training. Habits laid in the early formative years are difficult to

[11] Eleanor E. Maccoby, "Effects upon Children of Their Mothers' Outside Employment," in *Work in the Lives of Married Women, op. cit.*, p. 158.

correct later. It should be added that the difficulty of obtaining competent mother-substitutes will increase as more and more women enter regular paid employment.

From the short-range point of view, cooperative child-care, arranged informally among neighbors, seems to work out rather satisfactorily. Often, mothers who remain at home with their small children welcome the receipt of money compensation for the care of another mother's child while that mother works. But here again, there must be the assurance that the child-rearing atmosphere is similar in both homes. Then too, such mother-substitutes often prefer to continue their services only for relatively short periods, whereupon the working mother must find a new substitute. Too often such a situation impairs the child's habit formation and endangers his feeling of security.

The Children's Bureau of the U.S. Department of Health, Education and Welfare is one of the principal organizations among a number which have been working for more and adequate day-care centers for children throughout the country. In their efforts to secure better standards and practices in such care, they are demanding more effective licensing and supervision, better trained staffs, smaller groups of children, availability of counseling services for mothers, and recognition of the desirability that such services be community projects based in the community where the child lives rather than requiring long travel. It has been a matter of concern that in many large day-care centers, there are frequently too few adults to provide adequate care for many children so that a child may not receive the individual attention he requires either for his habit training or his emotional needs. Oettinger observes that in too many present situations the adults are too busy feeding, cleaning, and providing toys to help a child except when trouble seems likely to develop. It is true, however, that this objection to group care may be partially offset by the benefits the child receives from the freedom he can be allowed in a safe play situation, his association with other children, and the abundance of play materials proferred him. The best group care centers do offer many advantages even to children whose mothers are at home. But these best are hard to find, although their numbers are increasing.[12]

A matter of special concern has been that the dual job situations of mothers may result in emotional problems for their children.

[12] Oettinger, *op. cit.*, p. 147.

The reasoning has been that employed mothers are often unable to give their children the psychological responses they require, especially in the younger years. From the scanty scientific information we have had, the Children's Bureau has not been able to ascertain whether such emotional problems as certainly do exist among children are found more among those of working mothers, and, if so, whether such a condition is caused by the fact that the mother is working, *per se*. Here, as in the behavioral aspects, so many qualifying conditions can enter to affect individual cases, such as the kind of child, the kind of mother, and how the atmosphere of the home is affected.

We do know much about the basic emotional needs of young children. It is known that they vary greatly in the extent to which they are affected by separation from parents, especially from the mother. There are great differences in this respect even among children in the same family. For some, separation seems to cause little difficulty, but others become deeply disturbed. Such symptoms occur most often with children between the ages of one and three, before it is possible for them to understand an explanation of the parent's absence and be assured of the parent's return. In the words of Leo Bartemeier of the Seton Psychiatric Institute of Baltimore, "The emotional injury inflicted upon a child during the period of infancy has far greater effect upon his future character development than an equivalent damage experienced at a later period when his personality has become more fully organized." Doctor Bartemeier calls attention to the special function of the mother's attitudes and behavior toward her children during this vulnerable age in encouraging the development of the child's "innate pattern of personality."[13]

It was clinical evidence of this nature which led Doctor John Bowlby, Director of the World Health Organization, to present his much publicized views on the possible effects of full-time maternal employment upon the young child. His emphasis, after reviewing the extensive research literature on child-care over a thirty-year period, was that the *quality* of the parental care which the child receives in his earliest years is of vital importance for his future mental health. He maintained that when in the early years the child is deprived of maternal care, either by the mother or a permanent mother substitute, "the development is always retarded — physically, intellectually, and socially" and that

[13] Leo N. Bartemeier, M.D., "The Children of Working Mothers: A Psychiatrist's View," in *Work in the Lives of Married Women, op. cit.,* p. 175.

"symptoms of physical and mental illness appear." Bowlby hypothesized that one cause of the natural home group failing to care for the child is full-time employment of the mother.[14]

The position taken by Bowlby and others on the traumatic effects of maternal deprivation on the development of the child has stimulated considerable controversy and led to empirical research projects related to testing this theory. The peculiar situation of children reared in the Israeli kibbutz seemed to afford an exceptionally convenient laboratory for research in this area. Here, children live in communal nurseries with their age peers from a few days after birth to high school graduation, and are reared by nurses and teachers rather than parents, although they are allowed frequent visits with parents. As the child develops he is transferred from the care of one nurse to another in charge of an older age group. If separation from parents and changes in mother substitutes jeopardizes a child's emotional security, thought the sociologists, surely here was an opportunity to make observations. What, they asked, were the effects upon personality resulting from such rearing?

One of the most thorough studies of personality development of Israeli kibbutz children was made in the early 1950's by Melford E. Spiro, aided by a grant from the Social Science Research Council. His conclusions, based on criteria of creativity, curiosity about their world, sensitivity to creations of both nature and art, and their capacity for both work and love, was that the sabras (children reared in the kibbutz) "fell well within the range of normal human emotional adjustment."[15]

In spite of this general conclusion, however, Spiro noted among kibbutz children universal negative characteristics — especially a marked presence of introversion and insolence. He found introversion manifested in sharpness and embarrassment when interacting both with strangers and with kibbutz children of other ages than themselves, reservedness and maintenance of a psychological barrier with everyone, and avoidance of all emotional attachments or intimate friendships. He further observed that this personality trait was found also among the adults who had been reared in the kibbutz, in contrast

[14] John Bowlby, M.D., *Maternal Care and Mental Health* (World Health Organization Monograph No. 2 [Geneva, 1952]), pp. 15, 53, 73.
[15] Melford E. Spiro, *Children of the Kibbutz* (Cambridge: Harvard University Press, 1958), Chap. XVI.

to the ability of those reared outside the kibbutz to establish close rapport with others. They seemed to be "enveloped within a shell, from which their psyches rarely protrude, and which prevents others from penetrating beyond the surface."

In spite of these negative qualities, Spiro found in kibbutz youth a deep concern and sense of responsibility for others, and, most significantly, a strong need for affection and approval. The symptoms of withdrawal, then, he interpreted as a response to pain or anticipation of pain from disappointment in personal relationships.

In other instances, response of the kibbutz children in interaction with other persons was characterized by insolence, noted in such frequent expressions as "What concern is it of mine?" or "What concern is it of yours?" Both withdrawal and hostility were interpreted as psychological defense mechanisms — manifestations of insecurity resulting from deprivations of emotional satisfactions. Conclusions were that since physical care and training within the kibbutz child-rearing system appeared entirely adequate, the fault lay in insufficient nurturance, so that the child's needs for protection and love were seriously frustrated. Generally speaking, therefore, the main body of research conducted among kibbutz youth seemed to reinforce the Bowlby theory of effects of maternal deprivation on development of children.

With the extraordinary increase in the number of married women in paid employment, new research was felt to be urgently needed on the effects of maternal absence on the welfare of the child. This interest took the form of resistance to accepting conclusions such as we have just discussed, with the criticism that most of the research to date had been done with institutionalized children and those in abnormal child-care situations, so that results were not applicable to individual family situations. Consequently, during the past several years a number of programs have been initiated to study characteristics of children of working and non-working mothers.

Two new approaches can be seen in the recent research being done in this field. One is the shift in viewpoint to which we previously referred, away from a "child-centered" to a "person-centered" family philosophy — one which is, of course, more compatible with the role of the employed mother.[16] But convenience for the working mother is probably not the sole motive for this philosophy. Giving the child more respon-

[16] Nye and Hoffman, *op. cit.,* p. 6.

sibilities is good habit training. Moreover, we now pay more recognition to the fact that the well-being of all the members of the family is important to, and reacts upon, the well-being of the child.

Another new approach to modern research in this field is the study of children in sub-groups. Indiscriminate observation of children of employed mothers, without regard to socio-economic class, often reveals indistinct differences from children of nonemployed mothers. However, if characteristics of children are examined separately within selected sub-groups, greater differences can be seen. Nye and Hoffman report categories which have been effectively used as a basis for these sub-groups and suggest others that could be used in future research. Those which they employed are: social class; full-time vs. part-time maternal employment; age of child; sex of child; mother's attitude toward employment.

Recent studies indicate that further research is urgently needed on maladjustments of children as varying by social class. Little work has been done in this area except some studies on the relationship of maternal employment to delinquency. The results of recent empirical research here illustrate the value of a study which differentiates by sub-groups. From one such study, it appears that maternal employment and juvenile delinquency are positively related only in the group of medium socio-economic status. This discovery gives rise to the question of why this relationship exists in the middle-class and not in the lower-class group, and to further questions. Nye and Hoffman ask, for instance, whether the motivations for maternal employment, the nature of the work, and the attitudes of the mother and other members of the family may all be different in the two classes? In the study of both groups, Glueck and Glueck found no differences between children of regularly employed working mothers and non-working mothers except that women who work "occasionally" are more likely to have delinquent sons than those of either group. In many instances, the occasionally employed mother, they found, is more likely to come from an unstable family, or to be working to escape "household drudgery and parental responsibility." Family instability was often due to the father's emotional state or work habits, resulting not only in a disorganized home life, but lack of an adequate father model for adolescent sons.[17] Research on effects of maternal employment by social

[17] *Ibid.,* pp. 192–193.

class is needed to study maladjustments of children which are less extreme than delinquency.

The mother who is employed part-time seems to appear in a rather favorable light in the studies that have been conducted thus far. Not only does her working seem to have fewer undesirable effects than full-time work, but often it has distinctly beneficial effects upon her children's development. Such results are reported both by Nye and by Elizabeth Donovan of the Survey Research Center of the University of Michigan. Donovan theorizes that this situation may result partly from the fact that part-time, in contrast to full-time, employment of the mother may mean that the mother works from choice rather than coercion, resulting in her greater satisfaction in employment, which in turn affects the atmosphere of the home. Furthermore, part-time employment means that the mother has more time to devote to the physical and emotional needs of her children. Her feelings of guilt may also be allayed not only by this fact but by the assurance that she is less vulnerable to public censure of her outside employment.

Nye found that, in the aggregate, part-time working mothers had better relationships with their children than either non-working mothers or those who work full-time, although this positive relationship has thus far been found only with adolescents and has not yet been tested with younger children.

In any appraisal of the effects of maternal employment on the child, especially as related to part-time work, an important consideration is what makes the best mother. In these days of more urbanized living, continuous day-long confinement over a span of years to the almost sole companionship of children may prove at times intolerable, particularly to the woman of superior intelligence and breadth of interests. In such instances, part-time work when children are in school may benefit her in her approach to household tasks and her responses to her children. Some work outside the home for a mother who enjoys it can undoubtedly make her a more interesting and stimulating companion both for her children and for her husband. Such mothers must judge well the amount of work they are able to do within the limits of their time and energy. A fatigued and irritable mother will soon find things going awry on the home front, and her children will feel deprived of the parental responses which they crave. It has often been pointed out that the important consideration is the *quality* of the greeting and of the listening the child receives, not so much whether it occurs when the child comes home from school or the mother comes home from work.[18]

Some positive results can probably be claimed for the older children of the mother who works, particularly those in part-time employment who can simultaneously do a good job of organizing a household. One of these is greater responsibility and family function for the child, if demands on him are reasonable, as well as better cooperation among all members of the family — a wholesome antidote to the over-mothering that exists in some homes. One writer comments that "no one will delight in the prospect of a girl of ten mothering these younger siblings while the mother works. This is the sort of thing that should not happen. But family warmth and cohesiveness may be enhanced by assigning children responsibilities well within their capacity — provided the family setting is warm and healthy to start with."[19] Research has shown that the "early training of children for independence — to do things for themselves — shows a positive correlation with achievement motivation."[20]

There is also the distinct possibility that a working mother may stimulate her children to greater vocational achievement. While a psycho-analytic theory is that the child's self-image is most influenced by the parent of the same sex, there is also evidence that he identifies himself with more than one person, so that his several personality traits are derived from various sources. It is quite possible that the mother's interest in outside work also motivates the child. Eleanor Maccoby points out that a number of men who became noted scientists had mothers of outstanding careers and broad interests.[21] A study made by the Mellon Foundation at Vassar College arrived at a similar conclusion. It produced evidence that the most important factor distinguishing good students from poor ones is that the mothers of good students had intellectual interests and aspirations.[22]

But thus far, evidence of a positive relationship between part-time employment and parent-child adjustment has been found only with adolescents. Nye reminds us that we do not yet know certainly the effects of such employment upon the very young child and that the

[18] Oettinger, *op. cit.,* pp. 143, 144.

[19] *Ibid.*

[20] Maccoby, *op. cit.,* p. 157.

[21] *Ibid.*

[22] Mabel Newcomer, *A Century of Higher Education for American Women* (New York: Harper & Bros., 1959), p. 222.

definitive work in this area still remains to be done. Some recent studies have claimed that the mother's employment during the child's early years appears to have little observable effect upon the child in later years. This, for instance, is the position of Lee Burchinal, based upon his study of boys and girls at seventh and eleventh grade levels.[23] The team of Siegel, Stolz, Hitchcock, and Adamson claimed comparable results from a study of differences in dependence and independence between children of working and non-working mothers. Cooperating with a research group from Stanford University in obtaining data about kindergarten children in seventeen suburban schools, they reported that "one may surely conclude from these data that maternal employment *per se* is not the overwhelmingly influential factor in children's lives that some have thought it to be." However, they warn us that "this conclusion applies only to the age group represented by our subjects. One can not say what the findings might be if such a study were conducted with younger or older children."[24]

Nevertheless, regardless of the insufficiency of empirical research on this point, there is quite general agreement among psychiatrists that the young child, until he is six, has the greatest need for his mother being home. Nye reports, for one, the finding of withdrawal symptoms particularly in young sons whose mothers are absent. The need for the mother's presence in these early years is quite generally felt to be of psychological importance for both the young child and for the mother. Requirements of the child's physical care alone make the demands of a dual role burdensome and may easily produce in the mother feelings of guilt regarding care of the child.

With older children, there appear to be sex differences in their acceptance of the mother's outside employment. Positive results have been noted more frequently with adolescent daughters than with adolescent sons. The mothers in this category seem to provide an accepted model for their daughters much more frequently than non-employed ones, and girls show a tendency to choose them as models and want to work themselves when they grow up.

In fact, sex differences in response to employed-mother situations

[23] Lee G. Burchinal, "Personality Characteristics of Children," in Nye and Hoffman, *op. cit.,* p. 118.

[24] Alberta Engvall Siegel, Lois Meek Stolz, Ethel Alice Hitchcock, and Jean Adamson, "Dependence and Independence in Children," in Nye and Hoffman, *op. cit.,* p. 80.

have been observed at several age levels. Young sons of working mothers appear to be "dependent, more obedient, less self-reliant, less sociable, and more likely to seek succorance from adults," whereas "young daughters appear to be aggressive, dominant, disobedient, and independent." Other findings suggest that "sons of working mothers are withdrawn and overly dependent." However, these observations require statistical verification to be thoroughly substantiated. Hoffman stresses the fact that, if these relationships are eventually confirmed, it does not necessarily mean that the "father in working-mother families provides a weak model for boys," because "dependency and withdrawal are symptoms associated with maternal deprivation." She offers the additional suggestion that in the case of daughters the modeling principle may counteract any unfavorable tendencies resulting from maternal deprivation.[25]

Another suggested avenue of approach in the study of mother-child relationships is that of the mother's attitude toward her work. In this area, the few observations that have been made strongly suggest that when the mother enjoys her work, her relationships with the child are warm, so much so with the young child that her responses often seem to imply that she may have a guilt obsession. But the opposite interaction of the mother toward her child often seem to exist when the mother dislikes her work.[26]

The foregoing summary of research results in the relationship between the working mother and the child has been based on the body of reports gathered together and evaluated by F. Ivan Nye and Lois Wladis Hoffman. These authors specify that for the purpose of using manageable variables "only intact, white families have usually been studied," and suggest that, inasmuch as a sizeable percentage of full-time working mothers with children under twelve are not living with their husbands and another large percentage are nonwhite, research dealing with these two neglected segments of the population is very much needed.[27]

Hoffman evaluates the present status of findings on the effects of maternal employment on the welfare of the child in a statement closely resembling the appraisal given by Katherine Oettinger:

[25] Lois Wladis Hoffman, "Effects on Children: Summary and Discussion," in Nye and Hoffman, *op. cit.,* p. 202.
[26] *Ibid.,* p. 204.
[27] *Ibid.,* p. 209.

> Until recently the general view was that maternal employment had a great many effects on the child — all of them bad. Since 1952, however, research findings have challenged this view. But the pendulum has perhaps swung too far in the opposite direction and the new outlook seems to be that maternal employment has no effects at all. . . . The effects may be good, bad, or incapable of evaluation; they may depend upon a multitude of other considerations; but until considerable more research is done, we are not prepared to concede that maternal employment has no effects. . . . Maternal employment by itself is too broad a concept to be used fruitfully in parent-child studies and . . . in future work, test variables should be introduced to make this concept more psychologically meaningful.[28]

Thus, because each situation differs from another, the mother needs deep understanding of herself and of her child so that she can make an intelligent appraisal of the delicate balance between the requirements of each. But there is little doubt that the supreme test in her choice of working or not working must be that which will achieve the maximum well-being of the family.

This chapter was to deal with the *choices* available to young women in their future role as wives and mothers — the choice to work or not to work outside the home during the child-rearing period. We have tried to suggest some factors to be considered if a mother decides to work. Let us now look at the other alternative. The majority of wives who enter or reenter the labor force will choose to do so when their children are well along in school. Depending upon the size of the family and the marriage age, this will usually be possible sometime after the mother reaches the age of thirty-five, when she is still young enough for about twenty-five years in paid employment. Later we shall look at some of the factors to be considered with entry into the labor force at this particular time in the life cycle. At this point, we are interested specifically in appraising the homemaking role of these young women who will choose the alternative of excluding other major work activities for a decade or two in order to devote their thought and energies to the rearing of their families.*

May we not reasonably ask whether the modern emphasis on women's opportunities in paid employment is somewhat clouding our vision of the function of the home? Are not the status and financial

---

[28] *Ibid.,* p. 210.

* Some of the following discussion is taken from the author's article cited in footnotes 29 and 30.

rewards of the paid job too often upheld as the goals toward which women should strive at the expense of dulling their aspirations toward more intelligent nurturance and guidance of their young children? It is sometimes interesting and a little disturbing to ask whether the influence of the American home has not lost ground partly because of the frequent failure of women to bridge the gap between release from drudgery and the greater opportunities thus granted them for social guidance and intellectual stimulation of their young sons and daughters.[29]

So absorbing is the interest in future marriage and family for girls of high school and college age, that the asking of such questions seems to them to have no relevance for their futures. Their certain expectations are for a happy marriage and well-reared children. But it is often with the care of very young children — a period of relatively short duration with present life expectancy — that many women unknowingly begin to lose their zest for those goals that seemed more vivid when they were younger. They become blinded by the dull routine of housework and child care to the true meaning of their task, and confuse the mechanics of the job with its real and long-range objectives. They do not sense that the humdrum procedure of attending to the physical needs of the family is not any more monotonous or wearisome than the humdrum in some aspects of many a job or profession. They often lose sight of a vastly more important fact, that the daily chores of the mother are *only the framework* for performing the central and fascinating assignment of guiding the development of their children into mature human beings.

Admittedly, to an educated and reflective mother it may often seem that in consideration of the great need to solve today's social, economic, and political problems her homemaking role is particularly obscure. But homemaking at its best need not and should not be a cloistered occupation. As the child matures, the socialization of the home becomes an important and necessary goal, both socialization within the family and between the family and the world outside. The child needs to acquire understanding of and respect for those with whom he is both closely and remotely associated, a human quality so sorely lacking in today's world.

When the mother is free from feelings of guilt with relation to her

[29] Gladys Evans Harbeson, "Your Home and America's Future," *AAUW Journal*, LII, No. 3 (March 1959), pp. 147–151.

fulfillment of family responsibilities, she will be more likely to sub-stitute positive for negative approaches to child-rearing, being less likely to worry about the warnings of some educational psychologists and less likely to see her children as bundles of problems, even potential abnormalities. Unwarranted fear that a child may be suffer-ing from some blocking of his normal development has dulled the joy and stunted the fruitfulness of many a mother-child relationship. Thus, some mothers miss the rich experience of witnessing and en-joying the phenomenon of personality development. More emphasis on the positive goals of child-rearing can give a tremendous boost to the morale of young mothers.[30]

The late Alfred North Whitehead thought of the educational process as divided into three stages — romance, precision, and general-ization. He wrote in his essay, *The Aims of Education:*

> Education must essentially be a setting in order of a ferment already stir-ring in the mind; you can not educate mind 'in vacuo.' In our conception of education we tend to confine it to the second stage; namely, to the stage of precision. But we can not so limit our task without misconceiving the whole problem. . . . It is evident that the stage of precision is barren with-out a previous stage of romance.[31]

The creation of this "stage of romance" dominated by wonder, means a call to the child's inner nature, to the potential within him. And who is responsible for giving this direction to his development? Whitehead points out that the most important contribution is made by the mother, before the child reaches the age of twelve, so that when the teacher sends the child to the telescope to look at the stars, he feels he has been given "access to the glory of the heavens."

The painter, Millais, has illustrated this concept in his painting of "The Boyhood of Raleigh." Seated on a pier, beside the sea, young Walter Raleigh and another youth seem to listen spell-bound to a tale of adventure and discovery being told by an old sailor, whose outstretched arm points across the sea to the new and undiscovered lands of the western world. Indeed, may not the voyages of Sir Walter

[30] *Ibid.*

[31] Alfred North Whitehead, *The Aims of Education* (New York: Macmillan Co., 1929), Chaps. II, III. Reprinted with permission of the Macmillan Company from *Aims of Education and Other Essays* by Alfred North Whitehead. Copyright, Mac-millan Company, 1929.

have been inspired by a concept so implanted in his youth? The picture symbolizes the "stage of romance" in the education of the child.

To give children such guidance we need educated mothers. Too often we hear the statement that girls do not need much education because they are just going to get married anyway and not use an education. How far removed this is from the truth! To understand her children a woman needs the sharpened perception acquired through education. She needs the knowledge acquired through education to provide her children intellectual stimulation and guidance. Additionally, as her children become grown and acquire advanced education themselves, she needs a foundation for confidence that she can be respected by them as educationally their equal. Moreover, a fact frequently overlooked is that work well performed in arousing a child's interests and encouraging the development of his aptitudes provides countless suggestions for the mother's own growth.

Except in remote regions, there are relatively few situations today where motherhood must be an isolated and lonely state. Opportunities for some contacts with the community are always present. The many community services which depend very largely on volunteer workers seldom have as much help as they need. Unpaid community service is primarily the job of the married woman, because the time requirements are flexible and some such work can usually be conveniently combined with home duties. Then too, many jobs such as those with school boards, health agencies, churches, family welfare, and youth and recreation centers have important relationships to the well-being of each individual home. Here there are opportunities for service, leadership, and interesting associations in cooperative enterprises. In addition, participation in volunteer work makes community service part of an accepted pattern to the children, and if the mother chooses to undertake a paid job when the children are older, her adjustment to it will undoubtedly be greatly facilitated.

CHAPTER **6**

Which Roads to Self-Fulfillment?

*Sooner or later — and I think it should be sooner — women
have to face the question of who they are besides the children's mother.*

ALICE S. ROSSI*

Among educated women a new concept is emerging — *self-fulfillment.*
This can be seen as the culmination of women's century-long struggle
for emancipation. If this is its real significance, do we of the present
generation understand how largely our social environment is favoring
its advancement? How will we take advantage of this moment in the
history of women's progress?

Within the context of this development, what is the meaning of
self-fulfillment and what are the possibilities for growth of the individual within this concept?

We can better understand the meaning of this new watchword by
comparing it with those which have preceded it and out of which it
grew — *rights,* then *status.* During the periods when these objectives
were uppermost in women's thinking they were symbolic of the work
that lay immediately ahead.

Although the efforts to secure rights, both civil and political,
terminated in legal sanctions, such as those granted by the National
Woman Suffrage Act of 1920, the subsequent demand for status has
no date that can be cited for its realization. The ideal of equal status
includes recognition of women's abilities and of their equal rights to

---

* Alice S. Rossi, "Equality Between the Sexes: An Immodest Proposal" in *Daedalus.*
The Journal of the American Academy of Arts and Sciences. XCIII, No. 2 (Spring
1964), p. 624.

education, opportunities for employment and promotion in professions and occupations, and equal pay. Although progress toward this goal throughout the first part of this century has been impressive, much still remains to be accomplished.

Today, the concept of status merges with, and will no doubt eventually be furthered in its realization by the quest for self-fulfillment. This new emphasis is an acknowledgment of a woman's need to accompany her demands for status with the courage to be herself — with a belief in the value of her own specialized skills and talents, some of which correspond with and some of which differ from those of men. The idea of self-realization constitutes a more realistic approach to the goal of status.

The crusades for rights and status contributed largely to creating a new world of opportunity for women. Although prejudice still persists in many quarters, today women may enter the professions of their choosing. There is general acknowledgment of the fact that women in almost as large numbers as men are able to meet the highest standards of our colleges and universities. The opening of all professional and educational rights to women has saved for society special talents that in previous generations would have been lost because of prejudice. It has not only uncovered for our use the talents of such gifted women as Marie Curie, Cecelia Payne Gaposhkin, Eleanor Roosevelt, and Indira Gandhi, to name only a few, but a host of less prominent leaders serving their own local communities.

But in retrospect, the feminism which stressed the winning of both rights and status proved to be in itself a form of male dominance. The patterns and standards so long accepted as the norms for men were adopted for the evaluation of women's abilities, with little thought of special tailoring for women's own needs and for development of their particular talents. Male patterns of education have dominated women's education largely because "equal to" has been interpreted to mean "the same as." The process of educating women "exactly like men" has surely lost to us a priceless endowment which special talents and abilities of women could have supplied.

In the newer quest for self-realization, as the term is used in its best sense, there are possibilities that women may *find themselves by becoming themselves.* Anthropologist Margaret Mead comments:

> If we once accept the premise that we can build a better world by using the different gifts of each sex, we shall have two kinds of freedom, free-

dom to use untapped gifts of each sex, and freedom to admit freely and cultivate in each sex their special superiorities.[1] . . .

We can build a whole society only by using both the gifts special to each sex and those shared by both sexes — by using the gifts of the whole of humanity.[2]

From this belief it follows that women should rather be motivated by their natural preferences and qualifications than by a neurotic drive to compete with the opposite sex.

What are women's special qualifications and preferences? Before we can give an intelligent answer to this question, we must know much more about this matter than we do at present. The query opens an important new area for educational research. We know that women show stronger preferences for some fields of study than for others. However, we do not know certainly the full extent of women's aptitudes and capabilities because we have not measured how much their seeming preferences may have been molded from early childhood by social expectations and by custom.

Nevertheless, anthropologists are inclined to believe that there may be certain fields in which men will always take the lead and others in which women will excel. They point to the physical sciences, mathematics, and music as some in which men may have, by and large, a lead, while they postulate that women may have special aptitudes in the sciences involving human understanding. Again, Margaret Mead foresees the possibility of great social gains if we can learn to make use of the special aptitudes of both sexes:

Once it is possible to say it is as important to take women's gifts and make them available to both men and women, in transmittable form, we shall have enriched our society. And we shall be ready to synthesize both kinds of gifts in the sciences, which are now sadly lopsided with their far greater knowledge of how to destroy than how to construct, far better equipped to analyze the world of matter into which man can project his intelligence than the world of human relations.[3]

Self-realization, in its better sense, implies a paradox. As Harvard's psychologist, Anne Roe, has said, "It is only by making the most of

[1] Margaret Mead, *Male and Female* (New York: W. Morrow, 1948), p. 382. Copyright, 1949, by Margaret Mead. Printed in the United States of America. All rights reserved. Published simultaneously in the Dominion of Canada by George J. McLeod Limited, Toronto.

[2] *Ibid.*, p. 384.

[3] *Ibid.*

ourselves that we can make our greatest contribution to society."[4] Again, David Riesman, in a related idea, points out that "the value of 'togetherness' depends upon a continuing dialectic with apartness."[5] He reminds us that today we do not have time to meditate and that meditation is essential to culture. We need to take time to think what it is that we are most able and most happy to do, and to think how we in our choice can contribute to building a stronger social fabric. We must look both inward to our own resources, which education can help us discover, and outward to the fuller social uses of our individual gifts.

Thus far, we have done a very poor job of helping women look in either of these two directions. The result of this failure has been, on the one hand, an apathy and self-satisfaction in many women, and on the other, a frustrated and unrewarded search for a satisfying life purpose. Of these two, apathy and self-satisfaction may be the more difficult to dispel. This is the sort of attitude which has resulted in one type of women's organizations, of which there are too many in recent decades, where the only purpose seems to be gregariousness or where the organization has outgrown the vital purpose for which it was founded long ago. For the other group of women, who experience frustration, the pattern is too often a fragmentation of time and energies without significant achievement. For this group, however, there is greater promise of hope. Such frustration can indicate a struggle for transcendence of themselves. These women would benefit by realizing that it is better to do well one type of thing for which they have special ability than to divert their energy into many things for which they have little or no talent.

Again we ask, how are we to know our individual talents? Discovering the special gifts of young people and developing them for social use is, of course, the great central aim of education. Attempting some applications of this aim in the education of young women will be the purpose of the next two chapters. Here we shall consider only those general and differentiated feminine aptitudes on which anthropologists seem to agree.

[4] Anne Roe, "What to Look for in a Career," in *New Horizons for College Women,* ed. Leo C. Muller and Onida G. Muller (Washington, D.C.: Public Affairs Press, 1960), p. 78.

[5] David Riesman, "Women: Their Orbits and Their Education," *AAUW Journal,* LI, No. 2 (January 1958), 81.

The most obvious way in which women's special biological function affects their personality development appears to be in a peculiar adaptability for rendering service in the field of human relations. This demonstrated aptitude may well indicate a superior innate ability rather than a social conditioning for service in fields relating to the sciences of human behavior. It may also qualify women for bringing a distinctive contribution to the traditionally masculine occupations. As Margaret Mead suggests. "The mother, after giving birth to her child, must learn to project her feelings and understanding into the personality of a new individual. As she learns to attend to that individual, she develops a special way of thinking about human beings." From this hypothesis Dr. Mead deducts a challenge, that "We can leave these special learnings at the present level, or convert them into a more elaborate part of our civilization."[6] The ability which thus gives a woman understanding of her own family is needed in bringing understanding among peoples who constitute larger communities. Whatever other abilities women may have, here would seem to be an excellent area for feminine participation and self-realization.

Psychologists know that we have certain elemental needs which must be satisfied before we can transcend to the higher purposes of living. Abraham Maslow suggests a helpful classification of these.[7] He considers them all basic, although he finds some to be more urgent than others. The lowest of these, which are also the strongest, are necessary to sustain life, and until these are satisfied the others do not ordinarily manifest themselves. His arrangement of these from the lowest and strongest to the highest is as follows:

1. The physiological needs
2. The safety needs
3. The need for belongingness and love
4. The need for self-esteem and respect from others
5. The need for information
6. The need to understand
7. The need for beauty
8. The need for self-actualization.

[6] Mead, *op. cit.*, p. 383.
[7] Abraham Maslow, *Motivation and Personality* (New York: Harper & Bros., 1954), Chap. V.

Maslow finds that these needs have varying degrees of intensity and orders of priority in different individuals. All of the lowest continue in differing degrees of strength throughout the individual lifetime, but there can be little doubt that the needs for beauty and self-actualization have the best opportunities for realization in "the last of life for which he first was made." The greater leisure in the latter half of life should give women their finest opportunities for self-fulfillment. Moreover, we know that the drive for self-realization can transcend the more elemental needs in such a way as to produce an organized personality. This state we popularly refer to as maturity — the state of having found purpose and direction for our lives.

For those who prefer not to become gainfully employed, there is opportunity for self-expression in volunteer services. In fact, organized social agencies recognize among the qualities of a good volunteer the desire to put a particular talent to work. Social agencies in this country depend heavily on volunteer support. Without volunteer workers the services which protect our health, safety, and well-being could not be effective, perhaps not even exist. Almost five hundred national voluntary organizations dealing with programs for the young participated in the last White House Conference on children and youth. There are approximately ten million organized church women, and three million volunteers in Community Chest and United Funds campaigns. In 1961, the services provided by 28,000 agencies financed by federated giving benefited 81,300,000 men, women and children from all walks of life, and some 17,800,000 volunteers aided in raising federated funds and in managing the member agencies.[8]

There is an ever-increasing need for capable and intelligent volunteers in many areas of American life — in social work, recreation, adult education, and health services. Senator Robert Kennedy recently expressed the need by saying, "in my opinion, those who say there is no need for increased volunteer work in this nation have buried their heads in the sand. Our unmet human needs are so immense and pressing that they shame our national prosperity and endanger our position as a beacon to the aspiring nations of the world."[9] This is a day of many new pilot projects for helping the underprivileged to

[8] Giving USA, *A Compilation of Facts Related to American Philanthropy* (New York: American Association of Fund-Raising Council, Inc., 1961).

[9] Robert F. Kennedy, "What About a Peace Corps Spirit at Home," *Saturday Review*, XLVI (May 25, 1963), 63.

better help themselves. But achieving this orientation requires the work of high-level volunteers in initiating these programs.

True, many kinds of work which were performed by volunteer workers several decades ago have now been taken over by professionally trained ones. In spite of this fact, the need for volunteers has grown because of the growth of our population, the larger concentration of families in cities, and greater organized efforts toward public welfare. With the easing of work schedules through shorter hours and longer vacations there have been more men, as well as women, volunteering for community service. The growth of these organizations brings a need for a wide variety of abilities, from those helping to provide group activities in recreation centers to leaders of discussion groups and adult classes. Assistants are needed in hospitals, in diet kitchens, nurseries, clinics, and offices. There is need for help in fund-raising, in the spread of information — through newspapers, radio, television, and speaking before clubs, churches, and PTA's — as well as in providing new ideas for organization and procedures. In most of the larger cities any person who is interested in volunteer work can learn the particular needs in her area by going to the Community Welfare Council or Volunteer Bureau. Most of these groups not only place volunteers in suitable positions, but arrange for their training and supervision.[10]

Thus far, in thinking how women may use their gift of added years, we have not paid due recognition to another category of workers who will be fewer in number but whose self-realization will be one of the most valuable products of education. These are the women who can give the best expression of themselves through the arts. Some will find their truest self-expression and deepest satisfaction through creativity in music, painting, writing, and kindred activities. Theirs will be a lonelier existence, spent in endeavor to give their interpretation of life through their particular creative medium. Those so gifted may be giving us the highest order of service in their attempts to bring our understanding of life one step nearer to truth. Martha Graham, whose superbly creative artistry has expressed itself to thousands in the dance is said to have remarked: "There is a vitality, a life force, an energy, a quickening, which is translated through you into action. And because there is only one of you in all time this

[10] Melvin A. Glasser, *What Makes a Volunteer?* (Public Affairs Pamphlet No. 224 [New York: Public Affairs Committee, Inc., 1955]), pp. 9–22.

expression is unique and if you block it, it will never exist through any other medium and the world will not have it."[11]

To a few who spend their lives in such artistic creativity will come the opportunity of giving to the world a new and perhaps a valuable interpretation. But even those of lesser achievement in the realm of the arts may by their efforts encourage appreciation within their communities. This contribution to the understanding and enjoyment of life is a valuable end in itself, and may additionally inspire those who are more gifted to make their own unique contributions.

If education can first help our daughters to recognize their own individual talents and abilities, it must then inspire them to have confidence in the worth of their contributions to our culture. In these days of accelerated mechanization it becomes more difficult to teach the individual that he counts. Homer Folks, who so magnificently led the State Charities Aid Association of New York City for more than half a century and who in 1940 was awarded the Theodore Roosevelt Medal for his distinguished work in the field of social justice, well expressed such a faith in the power of the individual. He wrote:

> I have come to realize, as any thoughtful person must, that what any one of us does at any time, for better or worse, for much or for little, enters at the time into the current and texture of the social life of the community. It continues to have its effect, whatever that may be, indefinitely.[12]

A short time ago, Anna L. Rose Hawkes, as national president of the American Association of University Women, told an assembled group a story of a Japanese woman, which dramatizes this truth pointed out by Homer Folks.

In 1955 the International Federation of University Women planned a conference of all its Asian federations to meet in Manila. Inviting the Japanese delegation was a touchy matter because of the conquest and occupation of the Philippines by Japanese soldiers during the Second World War. But the Philippine women felt they could not

---

[11] Harold Taylor, "The Demands of Modern Society," in *New Horizons for College Women, op. cit.,* p. 99.

[12] Homer Folks, *Public Health and Welfare: The Citizens' Responsibility,* selected papers ed. Savel Zimand for the State Charity Association of New York (New York: Macmillan, 1958), p. 338. Reprinted with the permission of the Macmillan Company from *Public Health and Welfare: The Citizens' Responsibility.* Selected Papers of Homer Folks. Edited by Savel Zimand. Also with permission of © State Charities Aid Association, 1958.

humiliate the Japanese by not inviting them, so the invitation was extended.

As the conference opened the chairman of each national delegation was asked to bring greetings from her federation. This procedure created in turn a delicate situation for the Japanese. Mrs. Yamazaki, who had been chosen to represent their group, courageously opened her remarks by saying, "We have come here to apologize for the outrageous deeds of our Japanese soldiers." Her speech was favorably regarded by the press as well as by many Philippine citizens who openly expressed their thanks and admiration for what she had done. But Mrs. Yamazaki still felt grave concern. Her sensitive nature discerned the hostility which still remained among many of those with whom she came in contact, and this was borne in upon her most painfully in her meeting with a group of Philippine Gold Star Mothers.

On the homeward passage Mrs. Yamazaki said to her companions,

> We must do something to prove to these Philippine women that the things they suffered at the hands of our soldiers are not approved of by the Japanese people. We must show them that we are a people who want the same things in life that they want; that we want to be friends, that we have discredited our military and that we regret what happened. Wouldn't it be wonderful if we could invite them to come to Japan and see for themselves?

Her companions discouraged her for numerous reasons — the cost of such an undertaking, the impossibility of getting the Japanese people interested, and the certainty that the Philippine women would not come.

But Mrs. Yamazaki's determination did not flag. She talked to people, organizations, newspaper editors, and members of Parliament. She sought the aid of one of the royal princesses. Finally, the movement which she started was supported by 27 organizations and every big city newspaper in Japan. Within three months the Japanese women had raised 3,000,000 yen. They invited the Philippine women, they came, and as Dr. Hawkes comments, "the longest bridge of friendship in the world was built." She continues,

> Who can estimate the contribution of this indomitable woman and thousands like her all over the world? As community leaders, such women are invincible. Their education, their sensitiveness to the problems of people, their ability to organize, their willingness to cooperate, and their faith in

something greater than themselves make them think and stand together and choose to build a better world.[13]

Twentieth century American women can be deeply thankful that psychologists are beginning to express a belief in the unique social talents latent in the feminine personality. In our time, or that of our daughters, American women will probably come nearer to gratifying the fourth basic human need specified by Abraham Maslow — the need for self-esteem and respect from others, which we have more often referred to as status. With this prior need better satisfied, women can more confidently approach the gratification of the eighth basic need — that of self-actualization, or self-fulfillment.

[13] Anna L. Rose Hawks, "Developing Community Leaders," in *New Horizons for College Women, op. cit.,* pp. 64–65.

CHAPTER 7

Finding the Right Road

For some time now the socialization and education of girls has been preparing most of them for a world that has, in the United States and in many parts of the world, ceased to exist.

ESTHER M. WESTERVELT*

Formal education provides the opportunity to plan one's life — to map life direction. College women must ask themselves what do I expect to be doing not only two, five, and ten years after graduation, but what do I expect to be doing twenty-five years from now when I shall still have three decades of life ahead of me? Above all, they must ask how can I design my life so that the several parts of it — education, homemaking, employment — will make one integrated pattern?

David Riesman has termed the college experience a "moratorium" in young lives, a pause before commitment to a course, which gives young people time to discover who they are, what they have within themselves to fulfil, and how they can best make their lives functional within the trends of the period in which they live and the life chances of their social level.[1]

As educational opportunities have increased for an ever-widening segment of our population, it has become possible for most of those with ability to have a college education. But concern developed when

---

* From Esther M. Westervelt, "Counseling Today's Girls for Tomorrow's Womanhood" in *New Approaches to Counseling Girls in the 1960's*. A Report of the Midwest Regional Pilot Conference held at University of Chicago Center for Continuing Education. (February 26–27, 1965), p. 15.

[1] David Riesman, "Women — Their Orbits and their Education," *AAUW Journal,* LI, No. 2 (January 1958), 77–81.

it was publicized that the advantages which this privilege can bestow were being sought by too small a proportion of our young women. In 1955, a study conducted by the Educational Testing Service of Princeton, New Jersey, produced evidence that of the brightest high school graduates who were not going on to college, two-thirds were women.[2] And in a sample study of high school graduates, regardless of academic achievement, the U.S. Bureau of Labor Statistics found that only 41 per cent of recent girl graduates were college students in the fall of 1961 — a considerably smaller proportion than the 56 per cent of boys who went on to college.[3] In more recent years, this situation has improved somewhat. By 1964, the number of girl high school graduates going on to college had increased to 45 per cent. However, too large a proportion of capable young women do not finish college. Moreover, despite the sizeable increase in the number of women earning degrees, the percent of advanced degrees remains about the same. Only about 1 per cent of the degrees conferred on women were at the doctoral level both in 1940 and 1964, and the per cent of master's degrees for those years increased only from 12 to 14 per cent.[4]

In a later chapter we shall consider the implications for our national life of the under-utilization of feminine talent. Here, we are interested in probing into the problems and possibilities which the above facts suggest for the full development of young women themselves. Why do not more of our able young women enter college or complete their college education? Why is a college education increasingly important for women? What are the new patterns and viewpoints now developing in the higher education of women?

First, why are young women not entering and graduating from college in the same proportions as men? One obvious reason is that many of them still believe that they must choose between marriage and an education, but there are other considerations which are less apparent. In instances where the family cannot afford to provide advanced education for both a son and a daughter, the choice is almost always to educate the son. Not only is the son's education considered more important because he will become a principal family bread-

[2] Glen Stice, William G. Mollenkopf, and Warren S. Toegerson, *Background Factors and College-Going Plans Among High-Aptitude Public School Seniors* (Princeton, New Jersey: Educational Testing Service, 1956).

[3] U.S. Department of Labor, "Special Labor Force Report," No. 21.

[4] *1965 Handbook on Women Workers* (U.S. Women's Bureau Publication No. 200 [Washington, D.C., 1965]), pp. 179–184.

winner, but a daughter's education usually costs the family more. The President's Committee on Education beyond the High School reported in 1957 that 80 per cent of the girls, but only 70 per cent of the boys, received help from their families for the cost of their education. Only 4 per cent of the girls borrowed for their education in contrast to 8 per cent of the boys.[5] It would appear that girls do not wish to handicap their chances for marriage by debt or to transfer a financial burden to a husband, and are afraid they may not be able to repay the debt themselves before they marry.

But a most important factor in the unfavorable ratio of girls to boys entering college is that girls themselves have not seen the importance of continuing their education. Conversely, among the reasons that boys are entering college in increasingly large numbers is that more of them have come to realize the relationship between a good education and a good job and professional advancement. The holding of a good job has become more competitive as industries have come to appreciate the importance of advanced training for their employees. Our daughters have equally urgent needs for education, but are not as keenly aware of them as are boys, although such awareness may become more usual in the future.

What are the educational needs of women and why have women not realized them as readily as men have theirs? Among the strongly deterring factors are the influences in our present culture which are encouraging young women to retain a self-image which may have proved relatively satisfying a half century ago, but which today is shockingly out-of-date and misleading. Girls may well wonder why they need education for the kind of lives depicted on the screens and in the popular literature of our day. Moreover, advertisers, knowing well the effectiveness of emotional appeal, have added their influence to forming this stereotyped feminine self-image. The dominant figure in much of the advertising is the housewife, a happy little woman who is always beautiful and well dressed, but who does all of her own work. She has happy little children who are always either spotless or "sticky in the jam pot." Russell Lynes, writing for *Harper's Magazine,* has aptly described the advertisers' representation of the typical middle-class family. His "Highbrow, Lowbrow, Middlebrow" article appeared first nearly 20 years ago, but the picture is still accurate. The advertisers' image is of a world

[5] President's Committee on Education beyond the High School, *Second Report* (Washington, D.C., 1957).

without tragedy, a world of new two-door sedans, and Bendix washers, and reproductions of hunting prints over the living room mantel. It is a world in which the ingenuity and patience of the housewife are equaled only by the fidelity of her husband and his love of home, pipe, and radio [and, of course, television today]. It is a world that smells of soap. But it is a world of ambition as well, and constant striving for a better way of life — better furniture, bigger refrigerators, more books in the bookcase [often recommended by interior decorators], more evenings at the movies. To the advertisers this is Americanism . . .[6]

The reader may object at once that this is an extreme illustration which is not descriptive of the image in the minds of college women. But we shall return to this illustration shortly to show that it nevertheless points out some fundamental facts. An extensive study made by Elizabeth Douvan of the Survey Research Center of the University of Michigan indicates that social interests and the emotional drive toward marriage are almost exclusive in motivating a large proportion of girls to want to go to college.

In this survey, conducted among twelve hundred girls of all social classes who hoped to go on to college, Mrs. Douvan was interested in discovering what the desire to go to college *means*. The Research Center used vocational plans to distinguish three groups, each with different motives for entering college. It may be interesting for any college girl to ask herself if she belongs in one of these classifications.

The girls in the first group, comprising 13 per cent, were interested in some field of science or art, and were the ones most oriented toward achievement. The second group, approximately half the total number, comprised those whose interests centered on marriage and family goals, although work in the feminine professions still had some place in their plans. The girls in this group were more concerned with forming friendships than with their school work. The third group, 37 per cent, had very little interest in personal achievement and either had no definite vocational plans or sought the kind of jobs which do not require college training. They were most interested in friendships and popularity.[7]

[6] Russell Lynes, "Highbrow, Lowbrow, Middlebrow," *Harper's*, CXCVIII (February 1949) 19–28. This article has since been included in a book, *The Tastemasters*, Harper and Row, by Russell Lynes.

[7] Elizabeth Douvan and Carol Kay, *Adolescent Girls* (a study by the Survey Research Center, Institute for Social Research, University of Michigan [New York: Girl Scouts of the U.S.A., 1957]).

The picture painted by Russell Lynes and the images in the minds of about 87 per cent of the girls in the Douvan study have much in common. They are idealized representations of a romanticized feminine goal — the completely happy family pleasantly situated in congenial social surroundings as the be-all and end-all of feminine life ambitions. To young girls, a college education does not seem very important for realizing this picture, except as it probably increases their chances for making a good marriage.

If a girl finds her reasons for going to college and her vision of her future among the types just described, she may be sure she is quite a normal young woman. Perhaps the social scene is changing so rapidly, however, that these self-images will be outmoded in the near future.

The idealized pictures of happy home life are stereotyped and incomplete. They not only ignore the problems in family life which women must be equipped to solve, but there are no paths leading out of these pleasant localized scenes. Mr. Lynes has already suggested some of the facts which these mental pictures exclude. One which most concerns us here is that they represent only *one of the several phases* of modern feminine life during *only one of the several segments* of the total long life-span. One writer reminds us that maturity is not one of the highly cherished values in our society — that even the marriage counselors dwell on the emotional aspects of the early years, while life has also "long, pleasant but monotonous valleys" for which we must chart a course.[8]

Another closely related question which these pictures raise concerns the underlying values of women's lives. What will sustain women when life does not always measure up to the romanticized ideals of youth? When problems arise to be solved? When the relative leisure of the later decades begins to pall? Too many women, because of short-sighted goals, have neglected to develop their potential innate abilities to meet these situations. It is the function of a college education to help young women recognize and develop their personal resources, and discover values which will enable them to have fuller, more satisfying, and integrated lives. This concisely is the reason able young women need a college education.

College training can benefit women not only in the professions but in all their diversified roles. The sociologists tell us that marriages are

[8] Kate Hevner Mueller, *Educating Women for a Changing World* (Minneapolis: University of Minnesota Press, 1954), pp. 39–40.

more likely to be successful if both partners have equal education, also that education makes women better mothers.[9] The idealized image of a wife in the minds of college men has changed considerably in the past generation. A study of both sexes at the University of Michigan indicates that young people are seeking those qualities that assure good natural human relations rather than glamour in marriage partners. They want intelligent and understanding partners. In this study, good looks were rated lower than good dispositions, emotional dependability, maturity, and "well-roundedness."[10]

The mother-image is changing also. Somewhat dimmed now is the picture of the retiring, self-sacrificing, and completely domestic woman. The new image is a woman who is much more sophisticated and dynamic, intelligent about the world outside her home and a participant in it. It has always been true that where the infusion of intellectual and cultural interests into the life of the home has been fostered by women, the oncoming generation has been lifted to a new level where sharper insights have been obtained and purposes broadened and strengthened. The right kind of interpersonal relationships within the family are a strong influence on motivation for education, and this orientation of children toward achievement is established quite early.[11] One of the findings made by the Mellon Foundation at Vassar College was that the most important factor distinguishing good students from poor ones was that the mothers of the good students had intellectual interests and aspirations.[12]

The chances that a woman will seek and find employment tend to increase in proportion to the amount of education she has received. In Chapter IV, we saw that since World War II women are returning to employment after their families are older or grown. The type of position women can command at this age will of course depend upon the amount of their education. The following chart reveals the types of occupations filled by women with varying degrees of schooling (Chart V).

Even if a woman chooses not to enter or reenter a profession in

[9] Mabel Newcomer, "Women's Education: Facts, Findings, and Apparent Trends," *Journal of the National Association of Women Deans and Counselors* (October 1960), p. 38.

[10] Riesman, *op. cit.*

[11] Mueller, *op. cit.*

[12] Nevitt Sanford, "Is Education Wasted on Women?" *Ladies' Home Journal,* LXXIV, May 1957, p. 198.

Chart V. Jobs Women Hold Reflect the Education They Have Had

(NUMBER OF EMPLOYED WOMEN, BY SELECTED MAJOR OCCUPATIONAL
GROUPS AND YEARS OF SCHOOL COMPLETED, MARCH 1964)

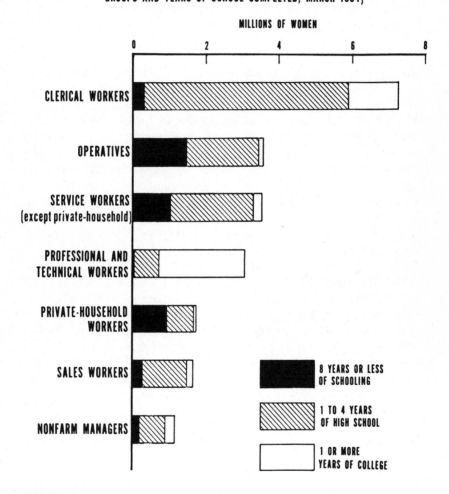

Source: *1965 Handbook on Women Workers,* U.S. Women's Bureau Bulletin 290, based on data from U.S. Department of Labor, Bureau of Labor Statistics.

later years, in one important respect she has a special advantage over men in using an education. Her freedom from the pressure of an occupation often gives her more time to savor and enjoy life, as well as to render voluntary social service. The arts hold such opportunities. Here, of course, she must have a will to achieve, for such personal freedom can result in a temptation to avoid responsibility and to become dilettante.

Since World War II, values and patterns in women's education have again become a live topic of discussion among educators. The concern has been shown not only by school and college administrators, sociologists, anthropologists, and phychologists, but by organizations concerned with education and the prosperity of our national economy. Among these are the U.S. Women's Bureau, the National Manpower Council centered at Columbia University and financed by the Ford Foundation, the President's Commission on the Status of Women, and especially the American Council on Education. Among the members of the latter organization are a variety of educational associations and organizations having related interests, foremost among them being approved colleges and universities. This group is a center of cooperation and coordination which has influenced the formation of educational practices for nearly the past half century. Its Commission on the Education of Women, initiated in 1953, concentrated its study not only on how to interest bright young women in continuing their education, but on the kind of education most suitable for them, its purposes, its content, and effective timing within the life-span of the individual. In other words, how can women be made more interested in education and aided in developing their total abilities?

In the midst of this controversy, a concept receiving increasing emphasis is that education must be regarded not only as *preparation* for living but as an *ever-continuing* part of living. It must be carried on simultaneously with other activities. This idea, which is receiving such wide attention in the education of both sexes, has special application for women. Both the lengthening life-span and the accelerating rate at which knowledge is now expanding make much of the learning acquired in the college years obsolete for use in later life. Paralleling this situation is the fact that in our affluent society, where only part of our time need be spent in earning a subsistence, we have time to continue our learning throughout the entire life-span. Dr. Mary Bunting, president of Radcliffe College, points out that education is fast becoming part of our adult life. She calls attention to the facts that the number of post-doctoral students is markedly increasing, that alert industrial managements expect in-service training of their employees, and that more individuals over eighteen than under eighteen are said to be attending schools and colleges in this country today.[13]

This trend in educational patterns holds much promise for partially solving some of the most vexing problems in the education of women. It may be increasingly possible for women to reactivate their skills in later years prior to reentry into a profession or occupation. Today, when women are marrying and having their families earlier, a large number of college careers are interrupted. Some anthropologists warn us that it might be well for us to evaluate this pattern of early marriages more carefully before we become too deeply committed to it. But as long as it persists, we must somehow deal with it in our educational planning. Even in instances where girls continue their education until they receive the B.A. degree, the interruption of the family years too often deprives them of motivation for learning and further intellectual accomplishment.

For girls with ability, what sort of college education can best lay the foundation for that which they can plan to continue in later life? Educators believe this function can best be performed through basic training in the liberal arts. Aside from the value the student receives from knowledge of the substance in such courses, she also receives training in ways of thinking and in self-discipline, useful tools in later life situations. Hopefully, she may acquire interests which will enrich her life and make it more stimulating — benefits which would be missed if she went to school merely to learn the technique of a job.

Formal education must prepare women for both homemaking and employment. With this fact in mind, we must ask in what proportions the liberal and the professional training should be acquired during the four years of college. Or again, if education is to be a continuing life process, at what time during the life-span is the more technical or professional training most useful?

Among the precepts learned through the educational process, one of the most important is that, although we may learn proficiency in a job, for its greatest effectiveness it is necessary to understand the

[13] Mary I. Bunting, "Education in Our Affluent Society," *AAUW Journal,* LV, No. 2, January 1962, p. 95.

social importance of what we are doing — to see its significance and purpose. Not to understand the social need our work may fulfill, or in many occupations not to understand human nature sufficiently to transmit to others the benefits of our labor, reduces the usefulness of our achievements. This principle operates both in preparation for family living and for other occupations. Various subjects offered in college open the doors to better understanding. Psychology introduces us to the working of the mind and to variations in human personality. English teaches us to communicate our thoughts to others. History and philosophy teach us what man has thought throughout the ages and how and why he arrived at his ideas. All of these and related studies in the liberal arts curriculum help us to understand our fellow human beings, to communicate our thinking to them, and to better understand theirs. Above all, we are helped to relate what we perceive as the purpose in our own work to the meaning of life. Otherwise, what we do in our particular area of training will lack direction and significance.

A liberal college education is the best means of leading the individual out of her own small world and interesting her in the larger one to which her life should relate. In thus widening her vision it also gives her insight into a larger choice of occupations for her specialization. The liberal arts help students to broadbase their lives and become more flexible-minded in meeting situations. These facts, of course, apply to the education of both men and women. But women especially must develop a general competence because the course of their lives is less predictable. With a flexible mind developed through a liberal training they are better prepared to adapt to the new circumstances which the inevitable abrupt transitions of the feminine life pattern have in store for them.

The timing of education for women is becoming a subject of increasing concern to educators. The prevailing opinion among them is that a liberal education gives women the most comprehensive preparation for being wives and mothers. However, it is thought that enough specialization should be included in the liberal arts course of study to equip them for holding the paid job that most of them want for the few years immediately following the college career. There is growing emphasis on the idea that further specialization beyond the undergraduate major is more usefully acquired in continued education during later years just prior to reactivating a profession or occupation.

Nevertheless, some specialization during the liberal arts course is thought to be most desirable for purposes other than training to hold a job. The college course should have a clear and definite focus. A study of motivation and achievement of college women recently conducted by Nevitt Sanford at Vassar College concluded that students with a field of concentration spurred by professional ambitions usually fared better in general studies as seniors and as alumnae than those whose primary aim was purely liberal education.[14] A field of concentration within the college course established a purpose for them, gave them a "point of application," as Dr. Bunting calls it. Some specialization is important also because it provides direction for the continued education which a woman may look forward to pursuing in later years. It also gives her confidence that she can at some time enter a profession, so that she can accept her occupation as wife and mother with more contentment in the knowledge that her domestic role is more a matter of free choice.

A few women's colleges, some of quite recent origin, have become well known for their innovations in programs especially designed for modern women's needs. As an illustration, we cite two of the older ones in this group which are particularly concerned with furthering this objective — Mills at Oakland, California, founded in 1852; and Simmons at Boston, Massachusetts, 1899. Among the newer colleges with this sort of interest are Bennington in Vermont, founded in 1932; Scripps at Claremont, California, begun in 1926; and Sarah Lawrence, Bronxville, New York, in 1928. Although Stephens, at Columbia, Missouri, founded in 1911, has been until very recently a junior college, it deserves mention because of its outstanding pioneer concept of educating women for modern living.

Mills College has a distinctly liberal arts orientation. While it endeavors to prepare young women for modern living by stressing both knowledge and skills, it describes its goals as "education for insight." Requirements for the Bachelor of Arts degree include experience in four areas of learning: science, the humanities, social science, and art. In the belief that there is "something creative in the outreach of every act of learning," the laboratory method is employed wherever possible and emphasis placed on creativity as a product of contemplation in all the areas of study.

14 Newcomer, *op. cit.*

Simmons College has a stronger vocational emphasis. But it was one of the first colleges in this country to recognize the value of combining vocational instruction with a liberal arts education. The first year of instruction is devoted entirely to general studies, followed in the later years by focus on a profession. The ten schools within the college provide preparation for most of the vocational areas in which there is a sizeable place for college women. The student devotes about three-quarters of her time to the liberal arts and sciences and the remainder to subjects of a professional nature. Considerable attention is given to counseling.

Scripps and Sarah Lawrence, both liberal arts colleges founded in the third decade of the century, are privately endowed and have comparatively small enrollments. Both have an especially high ratio of faculty to students, approach the planning of curricula from the interest of the individual, and give much attention to guidance. Scripps offers the student a rich environment of learning within the campuses of California's Associated Colleges of Claremont. The core of its program is a sequence of courses in the humanities, the purpose of which is to acquaint the student with the problems and achievements of man in the past in order that the student may understand the present and make her contribution to the continuing responsibilities of the future. On the other hand, Sarah Lawrence has eliminated uniformly required courses in favor of a curriculum planned individually for each student, and facilitates learning through small classes, discussion groups, seminars, and tutorial conferences in place of the lecture system. The creative arts — painting, sculpture, design, theater, music, dance, writing — are given an important place in the curriculum. Special encouragement is given both to independent study and to learning to live as members of a community.

Bennington, a college of three hundred and fifty students, also features individually planned programs of study leading to the bachelor of arts degree. Exploration of new fields of study is given importance along with building upon the particular capabilities and strongest motivations of the individual student. Here also, the arts program is especially emphasized. Bennington has a strong belief in the compatibility of general education with long-range vocational plans. It recognizes that specialization in the field appropriate for each student provides a strong basis for continued study in later years, and one non-residence term is frequently used to gain actual vocational experience or to test a vocational choice.

Stephens College began its program after making an extensive study of the educational needs of women. It keeps always in mind the probability that women will have three careers — early employment following graduation, rearing of a family, and years in outside employment after the children have left home. It emphasizes the "discovery of a socially useful vocation in a field of endeavor suited to each student's interest and abilities." The curriculum includes both functional general education and occupational specialization. Each faculty member has had training in counseling and gives guidance to four to twelve students. Stephens has a special interest in following up and aiding the progress of its students after graduation.

The rising concern to make women's college education more functional, which is so clearly evidenced by the recent founding of such colleges, is, however, shared by the older colleges throughout the country. Among the older eastern institutions Wellesley illustrates this interest. Although its central aim is liberal education, its program includes vocational guidance as a necessary part of the institution's role in preparing students to make a contribution to the modern world. The individuality of students is given much recognition, and the young women are given guidance by deans and faculty members in educational, personal, and social development. Wellesley has an efficient job placement program, follows up its graduates, and is one of a number of eastern colleges cooperating in the Alumnae Advisory Center in New York City in its work of locating college graduates in desirable job assignments.

Obviously, it is not possible in this brief discussion to give more than a few illustrations of the ways in which colleges are trying to adjust their programs to serve the needs of women in accordance with their changing life patterns. The counseling of women students is likewise receiving much greater emphasis in our coeducational colleges and universities. Continuing education programs are being established in many of our institutions of higher learning. The National Association of Women Deans and Counsellors used as the theme of its 1961 annual convention the topic: "The World of Tomorrow: Changing Patterns in the Lives of Men and Women."

In choosing the best college for a woman, an attempt should be made to match the student with the institution best suited to developing her peculiar interests and abilities. College catalogs will provide a good introduction, and visits to colleges will further an understanding of the particular characteristics of each school. One quality of a college is difficult to assess statistically or by a brief visit to the campus, however. An atmosphere of intellectual excitement and stimulation seems to exist in larger measure on some campuses than on others. Perhaps this quality can best be described by quoting Philip E. Jacob. These places, he writes:

> seem to have in common a high level of expectancy of their students. . . . It may be outstanding intellectual initiative and drive, profound respect for the dignity and worth of work, world-mindedness, a sense of community responsibility or of social justice, a dedication to humanitarian service, or religious faithfulness. Everyone, however, is conscious of the mission to which the institution stands dedicated, though this is not loudly trumpeted at every convocation, or celebrated in fulsome paragraphs of aims and purposes in the college bulletin.[15]

Finally, whether or not any good college or university provides a young woman with an excellent education will depend upon the student's own sensitiveness and response to the stimulation of the environment. For those who have the interest, the will, and the ability to learn, the possibilities are boundless, not only for a satisfying four years but for the lasting enrichment of their lives. Dr. Bunting writes:

> Further, the hope is that in the course of time there might emerge in the undergraduate a new psychology through which she would not necessarily look upon her married life as an automatic termination of her obligation to use her education extensively and meaningfully. Rather, as she senses the new expectations the world holds for her, she could come to think of the early years of marriage as offering new freedom and an unparalleled opportunity to experiment intellectually, to extend and deepen her understanding, and to explore as well as prepare for the interesting possibilities and choices available to her in the future.[16]

This statement voices a growing hope for the futures of young women in the concept of continuing education. Present opportunities and prospects in this trend will be discussed in the next chapter.

[15] Philip E. Jacob, *Changing Values in College* (New York: Harper & Bros., 1957), p. 9.

[16] Mary I. Bunting (pamphlet) *Unfinished Business — the Radcliffe Institute for Independent Study* (Washington, D.C.: American Council on Education, 1961).

CHAPTER 8

Following the Road

What we must reach for is a conception of perpetual self-discovery, perpetual reshaping to realize one's goals, to realize one's best self, to be the person one could be.

JOHN W. GARDNER*

President Bunting of Radcliffe has been quoted as saying that "if young women can continue formal studies on a part-time basis through the decade when the children are young, it may be possible for them to come out running when the last child goes off to school."[1] From the amused audience response when the writer recently used this quotation at a gathering of university women, she suddenly realized that, if taken literally, we see a picture of a woman ecstatic with joy at release. Nevertheless, this illustration seems an apt description of a woman who has developed a practical knowledge of the means for smoothly bridging the gap between two segments of her life experience — who welcomes the opportunity to use her cultivated skills in a still wider social context.

College educators report that girls are already looking somewhat farther ahead toward their later years,[2] and that the present generation of college students is less likely than those of the past to arrive at their middle years not knowing what to do with themselves and with leftover time to kill.

* From John W. Gardner, "The Servant of All Our Purposes" (New York: Carnegie Corporation of New York, 1959), pp. 1–2.

[1] Esther Raushenbush, in *Sarah Lawrence Alumnae Magazine*, February 1960.

[2] Harold Taylor, "Liberal Thought and the Women's College," in *The Education of Women — Signs for the Future* (Washington, D.C.: American Council on Education, 1959), p. 83.

To further encourage this forward look we need to moderate the American accent on youth which is so much a part of our present culture. Too many of the younger generation have been inclined to ask, with no small amount of foreboding, are not the college years the best years of life? The answer lies in response to another question — do we believe in continued personal growth? If we value maturity as well as youth, life gives us the excitement of a perpetual quest — continually expanding goals for self-fulfillment. This means, not living just from year to year, but, while we live the present to the full, also planning and keeping before us the objectives of the future.

This exciting process of growth can be a most enriching ingredient in family life. The personal orientation of parents toward maturity has a much more profound effect upon the motivation of children toward achievement than any amount of parental admonition. It can add a unique zest to family relationships. President Bunting tells of a visit from a neighbor's child during an evening when her entire family was engaged in study. The child remarked, "It must be fun to do your homework when your parents are doing theirs." A woman's realistic look toward her future can also make the present more satisfying to her through the integration of her own life purpose with the future objectives of her growing family. It can have the effect, as one educator has phrased it, of "planning for a life which accepts her femininity but is not limited by it."[3]

If a woman's liberal education has served its intended purpose, it has both lengthened her perspective and pointed out to her a field of concentration. This means that during the family years she may choose either to acquaint herself further with the area of specialization she elected in college or to inform herself in another field in which the broad-based liberal arts program may have sharpened her insight. This self-promoted study, during intervals snatched between various domestic duties, can form the bridge to her participation in formal refresher courses when the children are grown.

A number of means exist both for independent study during the family years and for more formal refresher programs just prior to reentry into professional, semi-professional or business activity in the later years. Moreover, these opportunities are constantly expanding.

[3] Virginia L. Senders, "The Minnesota Plan for Women's Continuing Education: A Progress Report," *Unfinished Business — Continuing Education for Women* (Washington, D.C.: American Council on Education, 1961).

Geographical location will, of course, be a factor in determining the number of programs available to any one person, but few situations exist where some such means is not available.

Before describing such opportunities in particular, it may be well to enumerate the various means now in existence as well as some which are in prospect. Two outstanding but differing programs for reactivating skills of mature women have been recently inaugurated at the University of Minnesota and at Radcliffe College. Both are conceived as pilot projects which, it is hoped, will lead to the adoption of similar programs in other colleges and universities throughout the country. College-level courses on television offer immense possibilities, which as yet have only begun to be explored. Still other avenues for continuing study exist in university extension courses and other adult education programs. The two-year community colleges, the numbers of which are now rapidly multiplying, offer for many women an opportunity to continue their education. Moreover, a topic which has been under discussion among educators for some time is whether college requirements might not be adjusted to better accommodate the life patterns of women by some changes in residence requirements and time schedules for acquiring the bachelor of arts degree, without lowering standards of achievement.

The first comprehensive program in continuing education specifically for women, known as the Minnesota Plan, was launched at the University of Minnesota in July 1960. It was made possible by a grant from the Carnegie Corporation of New York. Its organizers describe its two-fold objectives as follows:

(1) To return to the nation's paid or unpaid manpower pool at appropriate levels a group of intelligent, educated women whose abilities would otherwise be unused during their mature years.
(2) To increase the personal happiness of many women by exposing them to new interests, by helping them find new objectives, and by making the goals of the more distant future an integral part of their present lives.

The University of Minnesota plans to attain the above objectives through a three-fold strategy, designed to reach women during three different segments of their life span.

At first, undergraduate women are introduced to the continuing education concept through a seminar on *The Educated Woman in the*

United States, which analyzes such topics as manpower needs and educational resources, family roles, volunteer activities, and vocational planning. Additionally, a counselor helps them plan both for their near and farther futures.

The next phase of the plan concerns the young married woman. Upon graduation, any one of them who so desires is given the opportunity to maintain contact with the university by various means, such as taking evening courses in the Extension Division, correspondence courses, television courses for credit or otherwise. Even if during the family years the college graduate chooses not to work for credit, she is encouraged to use these facilities in order to maintain her competence. Since, at the expiration of the young-family years, she may wish to continue her formal education or engage some of her time in outside employment, it will then be helpful to her to have evidence of having continued her education on an informal basis. Accordingly, the Minnesota Plan has a record-keeping system to assist her. It will keep a cumulative record of her academic and relevant non-academic accomplishments which will show that her interests have not deteriorated during the homemaking years.

These two parts of the three-fold program support the central and most unique feature of the plan — reactivating the talents and skills of the woman whose children are grown. To accomplish this part of its purpose, the plan aids the mature woman to resume her formal studies. The small scholarships that it has been able to provide are often sufficient to pay tuition, buy materials, and arrange for child-care or some household help, thus making it possible for a wife to continue her studies while she maintains her home. In 1963–64, 92.4 per cent of enrollees in this part of the plan came from the twin cities and their metropolitan areas, 6.1 per cent from other places in Minnesota, and 1.5 per cent from out of the state. For this group of women, learning opportunities have been arranged which call upon the best talents of the staff from many departments of the university.

The response to the Minnesota Plan is demonstrating the urgency of the need it fulfills. Even in its first year of operation, the third phase of the plan drew more applicants than could be admitted. By the end of the year, 270 women had been registered. Their age distribution was from eighteen to sixty-two years, their educational background from the completion of the eighth grade through high school, college and master's degrees to one with a doctorate. There was likewise a diversity in personal objectives — personal enrichment, vocational up-grading, bachelor's degrees, and career shifts. Four were working for the M.D. degree and several for the Ph.D. Some were single, some married, and one had a husband and seven children. During the first four years of the plan, 1978 women joined the program, the number of new members increasing dramatically from year to year, with a contrast between 347 registrants in the first year to 686 in the fourth. In addition, well over one hundred young women had come to the center for counseling. The amount of interest in the concept of continuing education for women is further evidenced by the fact that by the completion of the third year the staff members had been asked to address sixty-nine groups.[4]

The Radcliffe Institute for Independent Study was established in the fall of 1960. Although supported by independent funds, it is an integral part of the college. In serving the cause of women's continuing education, its program is geared to a different clientele than Minnesota's. It aims to assist especially talented women who have found it difficult, often impossible, to continue their intellectual creativity after marriage. Usually they already hold an advanced degree or its equivalent in achievement or status. The essential requirement is that they show both evidence of achievement and promise in some particular plan of work. At the Institute, such a woman has greater freedom from personal obligations, a place to work and the facilities of a great university, and the stimulation of companionship with others who are working in various fields. It is hoped that in this atmosphere gifted women can prepare themselves to enter the world of professional achievement. As associate scholars, their study may be on a part-time basis. Most of them come from the Boston area.

From its beginning, the Radcliffe Institute planned to extend its services to other groups and to meet still other needs. One of these is to give to noted scholars, creative artists, or professional women engaged in careers the opportunity to spend a year or more in residence at the Institute. It is hoped they can be financially remunerated in accordance with their professional standing. Possible future plans also include conferences for women working independently in some sort of creative work, also for those engaged in such enterprises as banking and finance, urban renewal, or problems of immigration in their community.

[4] Women's Continuing Education Program, *Newsletter* (Minneapolis: University of Minnesota, Spring 1965).

Aside from the foregoing functions, the program is intended to conduct intensive research on the very questions that gave rise to the institute itself. It will attempt to find answers to such questions as the "nature and qualities of the educated woman's motivations and ambitions, her response to the difficult role of individual and wife, changes which might be made in the undergraduate education of women, both in method and philosophy, and ways to stimulate the educated woman to plan her life so as to use her education more satisfyingly and to build on it indefinitely."[5]

Like the Minnesota experiment, the one at Radcliffe inspires the hope that the presence of talented and mature women on its campus may encourage undergraduate girls to look beyond their immediate futures and to plan toward interesting objectives for their later futures as mature and educated women. Both institutions report that, to date, making the undergraduate conscious of her future needs has been one of the most difficult parts of the plans to accomplish. But also like the Minnesota Plan, the other parts of the program at Radcliffe have met with dramatic response. Its present expectation is to limit the Institute to fifty members, for one of its problems is to distribute its limited financial resources effectively. In 1963, its director reported that thus far the Institute had had almost ten applicants for every award it could make. However, it has tried to provide educational and vocational counseling services for the applicants for whom it could not provide grants.[6] Both ventures give credence to the assumption that many mature women are only waiting for the opportunity to make their education more functional in their later years.

Since the establishment of these two pilot programs at Radcliffe and at the University of Minnesota, the movement to enlarge adult education offerings for women at institutions of higher learning has been rapidly gaining momentum. Here, we can mention only a few of the most promising among this growing number, some of which are already established and others which are in the planning stage.

The downtown center of the University of Chicago has a series of courses for study concerning women in the modern world. One of them, *Potentialities of Modern Women*, concentrates on ways for women to increase and reactivate their abilities for use in the middle

---

[5] Mary I. Bunting, "The Radcliffe Institute for Independent Study, *Unfinished Business, op. cit.*

[6] Constance Smith, in *Education and a Woman's Life,* ed. Lawrence E. Denny (Washington, D.C.: American Council on Education, 1963), pp. 111–116.

years of life. There are courses in psychology for mothers, opportunities for creativity in the business world, and even a course entitled *The Nursing Profession and Economic Security.* Still another course focuses on role conflicts of women in a changing world.

At Rutgers, the State University of New Jersey, a program for retraining women in mathematics, supported by the Ford Foundation, was started in January 1961. As at Minnesota and Radcliffe, this is also designed as a pilot program which lends itself to emulation at other institutions. Stimulating its conception was the idea that the field of mathematics had developed so rapidly that women college graduates who had spent years in rearing a family would need not only to relearn what they had forgotten, but to acquaint themselves with new concepts and terminology. In March of the first year there were fifty-four women enrolled in the course. By 1963, most of those who had enrolled were still in the training stage, but nearly every woman who had received enough training to consider herself ready for a job had been placed. These newly employed women are reported to be happy in their jobs. Moreover, thanks to the bridge provided by the retraining period, adjustments in their homes have apparently been accomplished with relative ease and considerable skill.[7]

The program at Sarah Lawrence College, Bronxville, New York, aided by a grant of $91,000, got under way in the fall of 1962. While its Center hopes that many of the women it will serve will undertake full-time study, its primary objective is to assist women who are occupied with their families and who will be typically part-time students. It helps women who wish to resume their college education make plans appropriate to their purposes, and is interested especially in helping those with definite objectives find ways of accomplishing them within the New York City area. According to individual needs, the college may advise these women to study either at Sarah Lawrence or at other institutions in the vicinity.[8]

In response to a survey of 750 alumnae, the Margaret Morrison Carnegie College for Women at Carnegie Institute of Technology began working on a re-education plan for its alumnae in the fall of 1962. Over 70 per cent of those surveyed indicated that they were then in or about to enter a second career. The goal of Carnegie's project is to help its alumnae return to gainful employment, and, according to Dean Erwin R. Steinberg, the program is "not to be a

[7] Helen M. Marston, in *Education and a Woman's Life, op. cit.,* p. 102.
[8] Esther Raushenbush, in *Education and a Woman's Life, op. cit.,* pp. 105–108.

smorgasbord of adult education but a serious program of professional preparation."[9]

Among the larger institutions where ground-work is being laid for special programs in the continuing education of women are the universities of Wisconsin and Michigan. By the fall of 1962, the University of Wisconsin was far advanced on plans which were to involve the educational resources of the entire state. Part of its plan is the encouraging of senior women to continue in post-graduate training and prepare for employment by sending each of them a packet of materials emphasizing the need for trained women in the economic structure of the nation and providing them with scholarship and fellowship information. The University of Michigan began work in the early part of 1963 on a pilot project questionnaire designed to outline the needs of adult women for further education and the road-blocks they encounter in trying to secure it. From this survey, recommendations could be formulated on ways to facilitate the entry or reentry of adult women into programs of the university. At the University of Illinois a similar survey was conducted in 1964 through the distribution of over four thousand questionnaires to student wives and married women students. According to Dean Miriam Sheldon, in the 67.1 per cent of these which were returned, the respondents showed a prevalent desire or readiness for college work *now*, not at age 35 or later.[10]

Among other programs in continuing education for women which are in the making are those at the universities of Kansas City, Syracuse, Pennsylvania, New Hampshire, Florida State, Maine, Missouri, Marquette, Washington; and at Wells College and Colorado Women's College. Plans of this sort have recently been developing with such rapidity over the entire country that probably the best advice to women who are interested in furthering their education is to make inquiries about such programs at the institutions which are nearest their places of residence.

Aside from those institutions offering programs for credit, others too numerous to mention here are adapting to the specific problems of

[9] *Women's Education* (Washington, D.C.: AAUW Educational Foundation), June 1962.

[10] Miriam A. Sheldon and Betty L. Hembrough, *The Student Wife and the Married Woman Student: Their Educational Needs, Desires and Backgrounds* (University of Illinois, Urbana: doctoral thesis, 1964).

the married woman through non-credit courses which accommodate the housewife's schedule, and through counseling services, alumnae seminars, and publications of their alumni associations. Of course, this summary has not included programs established for a longer period of years, such as the law course for women, which has been in existence at New York University since 1890; Vassar's pioneer institute for secretaries, organized in 1956; and a special baccalaureate degree program for adults instituted at Brooklyn College in 1953.

Many women will be so located that they can become part-time resident students in such institutions as those we have described — resident in the community if not on the campus. But it is important for those who live at some distance from any such centers to know the other means available — correspondence with university extension divisions, courses offered for university credit on television, and for some purposes, the numerous junior colleges.

The work of university extension in all its branches is much more far-reaching and comprehensive than many people realize. Although it is carried on in such a variety of ways that the entire scope is difficult to estimate, we can get some idea of the size of the undertaking through the records of the formal university units which carry on this work. These programs are known differently as "division of continuing education," "division of university extension," "evening college," and "university college." Such departments usually serve to extend the liberal arts rather than the technical programs. Even in many instances where an institution does not have a separate general-extension division, arrangements can often be made to do work through correspondence and to use the library, or to contract for a research project.[11]

Television, which has already made such dramatic beginnings as an educational tool, has boundless possibilities in the field of continuing education. A report published by the Ford Foundation gives an idea of the scope of this development. Pioneer work in the field was begun by New York University in the fall of 1957 under the caption of *Sunrise Semester,* an early morning broadcast in comparative literature serving the New York metropolitan area. As early as 1961 this program, then in its fourth year, had an average daily audience estimated at 150,000. These courses are offered for credit, and include in the

[11] Renee Peterson, William Peterson, and Warren Roveteb, *University Adult Education — A Guide to Policy* (New York: Harper & Bros., 1960), pp. 58–60.

curriculum such subjects as physics, sociology, psychology, classics, and history.

Another institution which offers televised courses for credit on a large scale is Chicago Junior College. It gives the equivalent of twenty-five hours of college instruction every week. In the experimental period between 1956 and 1959, twenty-seven different courses were put on the air. The standard ones offered are social sciences, physical sciences, the humanities, biology, and English composition. From time to time, those offered have been in mathematics, modern language, political science, psychology, literature, speech, business, science, and music. During the experimental period, the semester average of those registered in TV College was 5,000 students. It is most interesting for us to note that two-thirds were women, median age in the thirties, mostly housewives who had been kept from continuing their education by home and family duties. Many of them were preparing themselves to be teachers.

Of course, one of the most dramatically successful TV programs has been *Continental Classroom,* which began in the fall of 1958, as a nation-wide course to bring about improvement in the teaching of physics in the nation's high schools. To this course, taught principally by Dr. Harvey E. White of the University of California at Berkeley, was added a year later a course in chemistry, presented by Professor John F. Baxter of the University of Florida. Still later, courses in mathematics were added, taught principally by Professors John L. Kelley of Berkeley and Frederick Mosteller of Harvard. Among the program's more than 400,000 viewers in 1959–60, there were at least 35,000 high school teachers. In the same year, these courses were offered for credit at 300 colleges and universities.[12]

For women who are unable to take advantage of these resources to obtain credit at a four-year college or university, another major possibility for continuing education often exists in a convenient location at one of the many junior colleges throughout the country. The founding of more good junior colleges, or community colleges, appears to many educators to be one of the solutions for accommodating the vastly increased number who are pushing for admission to our higher educational institutions. In this California has set an enviable example. While in 1950 all junior colleges in this country, both private

[12] *Teaching by Television* (New York: Ford Foundation, 1961), pp. 34–39.

and state-supported, totalled 506 and had an enrollment of approximately 244,000, in the fall of 1963 such colleges numbered 573 with an enrollment of 619,000 students.

According to a 1961 study by Leland J. Medsker of the University of California at Berkeley, the public two-year colleges enrolled at that time approximately one-fifth of all students in public institutions of higher learning in this country. About one-sixth of these were in the thirty-years of age or older category. Medsker concludes that "the teaching of older youths and adults to pursue college work will mean the continuous presence of many 'oldsters' on most campuses. This should be particularly true in local junior colleges where men and women with work and family responsibilities can attend college in their own communities without disrupting their personal lives."[13] This study showed enrollments in the business category heading the list, with trade-technical and industrial arts education a close second. The groups which represented a general education classification made up slightly over half of the total adult enrollment.

Of course, the location of educational offerings presents one of the most difficult problems for many women who desire to do advanced academic work. This is often the case for the young woman who marries before completing her college course and whose husband is transferred to another business location. As one educator has remarked, our young people are among the most mobile groups in the most mobile population of the world. This fact has been a strong influence motivating some educators to favor greater flexibility in the acceptance of transfer credits toward requirements for a college degree. It has been suggested that to alleviate transfer difficulties, some method of testing achievement in college work, possibly at the end of the sophomore year, is desirable. In fact, the Educational Testing Service at Princeton, New Jersey, has been working toward the perfection of such a device.[14] If at some time in the future such standardized testing can be developed to a sufficient degree of reliability, women will have been given another aid to continuing their education. But with so many opportunities even now available and rapidly expanding, the means for married women to continue their education are already abundant.

[13] Leland L. Medsker, *The Junior College — Progress and Prospect* (New York: McGraw Hill, 1961), pp. 297, 43–44, 74.
[14] Gordon W. Blackwell, in *Education and a Woman's Life, op. cit.,* pp. 75–76.

CHAPTER 9

Achieving an Integrated Life

In one of the most useful connotations of the word, maturity means that the individual has successfully come through what Erikson calls "the major crisis of adolescence, the identity crisis," and forged for himself "some central perspective and direction, some working units . . ."

EDNA G. ROSTOW*

As one observer has pointed out, women have now arrived at a crucial point in their long struggle for social adjustment, beyond which they cannot go without men's understanding.[1] However, it is equally true that they cannot go far beyond this point without a more adequate appreciation of their own capabilities. Certainly, the early leaders in obtaining higher education benefits for women never intended that the attainment of their objectives should turn college graduates into professionally frustrated housewives or socially unproductive middle-aged women.

The hard-won *rights*, then *status*, for which the pioneers of the past century crusaded now enable us to look farther ahead toward a newer ideal, for *self-fulfillment* has become the goal of this decade. But we must now press on to that which encompasses all of these — the concept of the *integrated life*.

To think of one's ultimate life purpose as making a social contribution, be it of great or small dimensions, can serve to establish

---

* From Edna G. Rostow, "Conflict and Accommodation in *Daedalus*. The Journal of the American Academy of Arts and Sciences, XCIII, No. 2 (Spring 1964), p. 758.

[1] K. H. Mueller, *Educating Women for a Changing World* (Minneapolis: University of Minnesota Press, 1954), p. 28.

direction. Here, we need to distinguish between activity, *per se,* and the underlying purpose of these activities. The procedure of a good teacher will illustrate this point, in that she will focus on both an ultimate and an immediate aim — what is to be achieved throughout the entire term of teaching as well as for the single day. The objective for the day must fit into and support the aim for the whole course. It must be *integrated* with the final objective. Comparable thinking ahead toward achieving a basic purpose can smooth the transitions in women's lives and prevent women from becoming either professionally frustrated housewives or socially unproductive persons in middle age.

The first of these are young mothers who, in the business of rearing a family, generate too much anxiety about their life fulfillment. Here they are, having had a glimpse of the world of intellectual and artistic endeavor during four years of college. And now? They are insulated from sources of intellectual stimulation, and instead, have a dull day-long confinement to the level of three-and four-year-old conversations. How logical, how fair is all this? Such responses are certainly not hard to understand and appreciate, but over-concern about extending personal satisfactions through professional usefulness outside the home too often results in tragic failure to glean the full measure of enjoyment and meaning from homemaking. Failure to understand the possibilities of coordinating purpose in the several segments of the feminine life span is partially responsible for the "futility literature" relating to the dissatisfactions of young married women, so prevalent in the past decade.

The emotional state of many of these young wives seems aptly symbolized in the theme depicted by a once popular artist. It shows a peasant woman fording a shallow stream with a wagon load of poultry which she is taking to market. Aggravated beyond reason by the slow progress of the little donkey pulling the cart, the woman with whip in hand is lashing the beast to speed him to the opposite bank of the stream. At the same time, unknown to her, the feathered flock which are the purpose of her journey are escaping in a wild flutter through the accidentally unlatched door at the back of the wagon.

The second group who would benefit by long-range planning are the women who arrive at middle age without having been concerned *enough* about their life objectives and without having looked ahead. Or, having arrived at middle age, they experience serious difficulties in making the transition from motherhood to broader social use-fulness. Ministers, doctors, lawyers — those whose professions give them insights into personal lives — know that there are an appalling number of unhappy women over forty. They also know that many of these could be helped if they could find sufficient purpose for their lives. These women are simply at a loss to know what to do with themselves when they reach the point where their children are no longer dependent upon them. Usually, these are ones who have been the most devoted mothers. Not a few of them feel a quiet desperation in their desire to be of greater usefulness, but are at a loss to know how. They have not foreseen what their later years would be like and have not planned for them. Their only relief is in some form of occasional social diversion which provides them escape. Integration of the several parts of their lives has not been achieved.

Full self-realization during both the family years and the later life-span need not imply contradiction. This point is particularly important for the impatient young mother to remember. In fact, the first years should in one respect equip and qualify her for the later ones. As we have previously noted, women's ordained physical function in perpetuating the race fosters in them psychological apti-tudes conditioning them more fully than the male sex for protecting and caring for the young. These qualities of outer-directedness can later be of immense usefulness in the larger social environment outside the home. When women's emancipation becomes more fully realized and its significance more apparent, we may come to know what Margaret Mead has tried to help us understand, that the discipline of unalterable biological facts creates in women some of the very aptitudes needed to bring about better social relationship among discordant elements in our society.

If her experiences as a wife and mother have been well used, what is the woman of thirty-five or forty like? She both knows, and is known in, her community. She has energy. She has wisdom gleaned from experience. She has learned to look outward and to live for others; to look into other people's lives with penetrating understand-ing and, one would hope, a warm sympathy. Because of these qualities she can be of inestimable value to her community. To waste these gifts at this high point of personal development, with all their poten-tial for good, is utter personal and social prodigality.

Attaining a satisfying and productive life pattern for the mature women cannot be accomplished by women alone; we must have the interest and cooperation of men. A militant approach, paralleling the earlier crusades for rights, is surely not the best method of securing wider recognition. Allowing for the existence of some degree of prejudice and selfishness in reserving jobs for men, women must effect progress in large measure today by bringing to men a better understanding of the modern woman's situation. As one French writer has so aptly said, the images which people form of the status of women in relation to different social structures can either delay or accelerate changes in their actual status. Furthermore, he adds, "What good would it do man to maintain his 'superiority' and what good would it do woman to gain her 'freedom' if in doing so they felt themselves strangers to one another? This is why it is so important for the future that the two sexes should adopt a common guiding image."[2]

Among reasons listed for hesitancy to employ and promote women are: that women's skills become rusty during the family-rearing years; that their obligations as wives and mothers affect their attitudes and work behavior. Too often they do not give their work priority. Special problems arise, such as not being able to move away from families, not wishing to travel, and leaving the job for periods of from two to five years. Women require special accommodations. It is expensive for management to have to install separate facilities and in some instances even provide transportation. With regard to promotions, employers say that absenteeism among women prevents their complete integration into the job-promotion ladder.[3]

In addition to male employers being made acquainted with the dilemma of the middle-aged woman and of the social waste among women in this age bracket, they should be persuaded to become more objective in hiring and promoting — that is, not to allow their opinion of work behavior of all women to be influenced by the unsatisfactory performance of a few, but rather to judge the merits of each woman employee on an individual basis.

On the other hand, women must meet objections where they are well founded. If a woman's work attitude and behavior are too

[2] P. Chombart de Lauwe, "Images of Women in Society," *International Social Science Journal* (UNESCO), XIV (1962), p. 23.

[3] National Manpower Council, *Womanpower* (New York: Columbia University Press, 1957), pp. 88–97.

strongly affected by her duty to her family, then she should either postpone outside employment until the family life cycle reaches a point where her home responsibilities are lightened, or else not resent being overlooked among the promotions. If her skills have become rusty during the family years, she should seek training to equip her for the job. If employers can be persuaded to judge her work on an individual basis, then the woman's right to promotion would become her own responsibility to prove, even though she might have to work harder at proving it than a man. For instance, she may be able to disprove the claim of too frequent absenteeism and distractions because of family situations. But facts, such as her inability to gain promotion because her family relationship keeps her from moving to another community, or the extra expense of special accommodations, have to be accepted without resentment. There must be greater honesty and a more realistic approach on the part of both employer and employee. There should also be programs of research and honest bi-partisan appraisal of these problems within local communities. Mutual respect would more likely be encouraged by an unemotional and more objective approach.

In addition to these well-founded objections to employing women, there are others which stand on the shadowy boundary between truth and fiction. Among these, we have to face a deep-rooted tradition of distinction between "men's" and "women's" jobs. Employers claim that this situation is not entirely a case of following their own opinions, but of catering to the public's expectations of whom they expect to find in certain positions. And as to job promotions, the opinion is quite prevalent that neither men nor women like to work for women supervisors. These are all ideas related to the belief held by employers, the general public, and often by women themselves that women possess well-defined traits and abilities which qualify or disqualify them for certain kinds of work. We have noted some seemingly well-founded justifications for these opinions; however, feminine qualities have frequently not been accurately assessed.

An additional complaint on the part of employers is that the hiring of women increases labor costs, especially in job training and pensions. Many employers are unwilling to invest in training women because they feel uncertain how long they will be willing to remain with the job.[4] These are among the considerations which at present form

4 *Ibid.*

a clouded picture, and which consequently invite study and investigation. A concerted approach is being made by the U.S. Department of Labor, through its Women's Bureau, Bureau of Labor Statistics, and Bureau of Employment Security toward the investigation of such claims, and, wherever such accusations prove false, to countering them.

For their own protection, and for an awareness of advances in the cause of the employed woman, women should have at least a general knowledge of what has already been achieved for them through legislation, and why. Although women in this country have shared with men the protection and advantages of regulations adopted for the benefit of all workers, early special legislation for women was enacted, designed to protect mostly those from lower-income groups in factory and office jobs. Such laws have regulated conditions of work, hours of work in certain industries and occupations, day of rest, meal and rest periods, night work, and minimum wages. Some or all of these are on the statute books of almost all states in the Union. As of September 1, 1965, a total of 34 states, the District of Columbia, and Puerto Rico had minimum wage laws with minimum wage rates currently in effect. As of the same date, 25 states had equal pay laws.[5]

Today, there are new problems and demands growing out of recent social change. One of the most unique developments is the influx into the labor market of those from higher social and economic strata, a phenomenon furthered by the multiplication of office jobs. This change in the social stratification of workers creates new types of needs of which the educated woman in employment situations should be aware. The *Wall Street Journal* comments: "Helping the woman-to-work trend, of course, is the fact that the country is shifting from a civilization of shovellers and sledge hammer wielders to one of paper shufflers. A woman is slow with the sledge hammer. But she shuffles papers as nimbly as a man — often more so."[6]

Highlighting the increasing interest of women from higher income groups in job-holding is a survey recently reported in the *New York Times*. Interviews with two hundred college-trained housewives in the distinctly upper-income area of Westchester County, New York, revealed that more than 50 per cent of these women in the twenty-five to thirty-five year old bracket wanted paid employment at the

[5] *1965 Handbook on Women Workers* (U.S. Women's Bureau Publication No. 290 [Washington, D.C.]), pp. 235–238.
[6] *Wall Street Journal* (Chicago edition), April 10, 1962.

time of the survey or within the next five to fifteen years. Only 32 per cent were sure they would not work again for gain. This was true in spite of the fact that 62 per cent were already doing volunteer work. A third of these had married at age twenty or under, and more than half had married under twenty-three. Many of their children were in boarding school or old enough to require less parental care. Either experiencing or anticipating the dawning of a new freedom from family obligations, their problem was what to do with it. Seventy-five per cent of those interviewed thought their education was inadequate and 80 per cent planned to return to school. The report comments, "after ten years of the charcoal grill, the school car pool and the daily bath for the 7:40, there appears to be a growing unrest among the women of suburbia. It is shown most clearly in the desires of many suburban women to return to full-time or part-time jobs."[7]

Here, incidentally, is an apt illustration of how a changed public opinion with regard to the fitness of women for paid jobs as well as the fitness of certain jobs for women, is emerging. With few exceptions, women in this upper level of social stratification would not have expressed interest in paid employment even a decade or two ago. But improvements in status, opportunities, and working conditions for women have encouraged the large-scale employment of those from upper-income groups. Dr. Gertrude Bancroft, speaking to members of the American Economic Association as early as 1959 declared that it was becoming "quite socially correct" for wives of upper-income husbands to hold paid jobs. She pointed out that, for some years preceding, the increase in labor force activity of women had been at the upper end of the income scale.[8]

Part-time jobs and work for those over forty will be some of the increasing demands growing out of this seeking of paid employment by women of higher social status. Part-time employment is defined by the U.S. Bureau of the Census as a workweek of one to thirty-four hours. Recent investigations of the President's Commission on the Status of Women revealed that inflexibility regarding part-time employment, both in government and private enterprise, is at present excluding from productive work many able women, including highly trained professionals who, because of family commitments, can work

---

[7] *New York Times*, April 3, 1960, p. 81.

[8] *Ibid.*, December 28, 1959, p. 25.

only part-time. The Commission recommended that hiring practices be altered to permit more part-time work.[9]

In spite of much reluctance to adjusting time-schedules, part-time employment of women has already shown considerable increase. In 1950, only one out of four employed women worked part time; in 1962, the number was one out of three. Most of these are women with family responsibilities, college students, and partially disabled or older workers. And in 1962, three-fifths of all part-time work was done by women. It was the opinion of the President's Commission that "part-time work is particularly important for women; it is sometimes seen as the solution to their problem of balancing home, community, and job responsibilities." During the course of the Commission's conducting their investigations, fifteen government agencies in Washington supplied them with information about their part-time workers. All of them reported that they found these workers at least as productive as their full-time help; one agency commented that the part-time helper was usually overqualified for the specific assignment.[10]

In addition to the above recommendations, the Commission urged women to seek part-time employment through placement services in their professional associations, and to make application for jobs at particular institutions and agencies. The largest number of part-time workers are reported to be teachers in elementary and secondary schools and colleges, librarians, professional nurses, and workers in other branches of the health services — occupational and physical therapists, dietitions, dental hygienists, medical technologists, and medical x-ray technicians. Part-time positions for dental hygienists in private dental offices are reported as particularly numerous and well paying. Part-time employment in social work presents many openings largely because of the shortage of full-time workers in this field.

Additionally, there are part-time jobs in such professional fields as art, writing, designing, entertaining, photography, athletics, sports instruction, and in welfare and religious work. Newspaper writing is an occupation offering an unusually good market for part-time workers because of the variety of assignments, opportunities for free-lance writing, and flexible hours.

[9] *American Women.* The Report of the President's Commission on the Status of Women (New York: Charles Scribner's Sons, 1965), p. 211.
[10] *Ibid.*

In addition to work in the foregoing categories, many find part-time employment as managers, officials, and proprietors. Many of these are self-employed. The opportunities in such fields include jobs as buyers and proprietors in retail trade; managers of apartment houses and cafeterias; bankers; postmistresses; program directors for radio and television; and cateresses.

For those trained for work of a clerical nature, there are many opportunities for part-time work as secretaries, although both secretaries and stenographers are usually hired on a full-time basis. Most part-time opportunities here are usually in doctors' and dentists' offices, welfare and religious services, non-profit membership organizations, etc. Those doing part-time work in their homes on theses, manuscripts, and form letters are also counted in this group.

Other part-time positions in the list of clerical occupations include those in banks as proofing machine operators and as cashiers for various kinds of services. Operators of profing machines are employed to meet the peak load at the end of banking hours. The skill required here in listing and sorting checks can be acquired in a relatively short time with on-the-job training.

It should be encouraging to married women seeking employment that the present market for part-time workers is expected to expand within the next decade, to a total of nine million women by 1975. This forecast is of course contingent upon probable changes such as new legislative action, union-management agreements, changes in school attendance patterns or in working-life patterns of women, and the number of part-time jobs made available in various occupations and industries.[11]

Another hopeful trend is the increasing demand for over-forty workers. The nation's need for additional trained manpower has been responsible for lessening resistance to the employment of this group of workers; the trend has been promoted by efforts of the U.S. Department of Labor to encourage wider use of people in this age bracket whose skill and experience have been heretofore under-utilized. The increasing availability for paid employment of women whose children are grown has added impetus to the Department's efforts to dispel prejudice against this group of workers.

With the need for trained labor from upper-age brackets increasing,

[11] *Part-time Employment for Women* (U.S. Women's Bureau Publication No. 273 [Washington, D.C., 1960]), pp. 1–7.

one problem now is that hiring restrictions exist in many occupations, and that these arbitrary limitations can seriously affect the use of millions of experienced and trained workers. Those in the upper-age groups who have the greatest difficulty finding employment are those who have been out of a job for some time. Women who have been out of work because of rearing a family are, of course, included in this group.

In a couple of surveys conducted by the National Office Management Association in 1957 and 1958, it was found that 42 per cent of the companies investigated had age requirements set at fifty or below for men, and that an even higher percentage had such restrictions for women. But progress toward fuller manpower utilization here began shortly after this date. In August 1961, Arthur J. Goldberg, then Secretary of Labor, reported that a Senate sub-committee had found that, while in 1956 fifty per cent of all job openings in five areas had restrictive age requirements, by 1961 the figure had dropped to 39 per cent.[12] In recent years, the U. S. Department of Labor has conducted research on the validity of claims upon which these restrictions have been based. Their research highlights the fact that much of the belief about low productivity of older workers is unfounded. Many workers over fifty-five were found to have output rates which were actually higher than the average rate in the group of peak production, In clerical studies, workers in the older age groups had a steadier rate of output, with considerably less variation from week to week, than workers in the younger age groups.[13]

In addition to these findings on productivity, notations on other results in this same study must be made. Relatively twice as many older job seekers as younger ones were classified as skilled workers. Many of the older workers demonstrated in their work histories an ability to shift occupational fields. In the Department's report of the results of a couple of surveys by national business associations, half to three-fifths of the employers interviewed thought that the older worker is more difficult to train for specific jobs. However, the opinion was expressed by a majority that once trained, the older men and women performed as well as, if not better than, workers under fifty. In addition to the advantages of skill and experience, older workers were found

[12] *New York Times,* August 25, 1961, p. 49.
[13] *Meet the Over 40 Worker* (U.S. Department of Labor Special Publication [Washington, D.C., 1960]), p. 11.

to have greater stability and tended to stay with the job longer than younger ones. Moreover, they had greater ability to meet the public and, because they were usually more knowledgeable, they were found to inspire confidence and respect. The Department of Labor believes that employers should consider the entire package of benefits in hiring older workers.[14]

Among the most realistic deterrents to the employment of women in some locations have been a group of problems related to disability payments and pensions, the latter due to the shorter span of employment than men's in later years. The childbearing, childrearing, and homemaking functions of younger women, of course, create special problems in the former area. But, because significant changes in women's work have been developing since the middle of the nineteenth century, we have come to realize that the nation's best interests demand good labor standards for women. Large numbers of women workers in this country are now eligible to receive maternity benefits. These are provided generally through voluntary health and insurance plans or by legislative action varying according to states. Voluntary health plans include those negotiated between unions and management, those offered by commercial insurance companies, those operated by associations of hospitals or physicians, and those operated cooperatively by groups.[15] Among the standards recommended by the U.S. Department of Labor are sick leave and maternity leave without loss of job or seniority rights — maternity leave to cover a minimum of six weeks before and two months after confinement — and paid maternity leave or comparable insurance benefits for women workers.[16] Of course, although such measures provide an over-all gain, the possibilities of having to provide such compensation contributes further to the hesitancy of some employers to recruit married women workers.

These are some of the considerations about which women seeking employment should be knowledgeable in order to better understand the responses they will experience from some employers.

But the growing demand for more intelligent and trained workers in paid employment is only part of our need for workers. The call for volunteers is also becoming more urgent. It is feared that the siphoning off of women workers into gainful employment will create serious shortages in the volunteer agencies. Fortunately, many women will

[14] *Ibid.,* 18.
[15] *1965 Handbook on Women Workers, op. cit.,* p. 51.
[16] *Ibid.,* p. 230.

prefer to work in these areas. In fact, there are increasingly more volunteers in our country today as people acquire more leisure. But the scope of these services has expanded so greatly that we have a shortage of personnel in almost every role.

Although many of our younger educated women find such work congenial, annual reports received in the office of the American Association of University Women show that volunteering in the United States still involves mostly the woman in the middle-income bracket in the years after her children are grown and before her husband retires. The reports show additionally that agencies can use all the special skills the community can provide.[17]

We would like to quote here a statement made by Secretary Ribicoff of the United States Department of Health, Education, and Welfare in a speech at the headquarters of the Educational Foundation of the American Association of University Women. To the assembled representatives of volunteer agencies he said:

> We need you, the American volunteer. . . . We need your help in the months and years ahead. But to this I add a special request: We ask you to pause for a bit from your busy activities to reflect upon your role and your potential in American life, so that we may make the best possible use of the precious volunteer manhour and . . . accomplish the greatest possible good.[18]

Basing their programs on research at the national level by both government and educational institutions, some of our women's organizations should be able to make a substantial contribution in their own localities by investigating certain aspects of the problems we have here discussed. They could conduct surveys of local employment needs and practices and of the number of mature women who desire work, either on a paid or voluntary basis, part-time or full-time, outside the home. Any such roster of women, specifying work experience, education, willingness to receive training to up-date their skills, locations and hours of work desired, could be made available for the use of both employers and prospective applicants. Also, whether or not employers are interested in such a project, records could be secured from them on their past experience in employing women.

In this connection, one important function of organized groups

17 Edith H. Sherrard, "The Changing Volunteer in a Changing Society," *AAUW Journal*, LV, No. 2 (January 1962), pp. 88–91.
18 *Ibid.*

would be to disseminate knowledge of women's present situation in our changing society. Any attempts to widen opportunities for women should be prefaced with efforts to acquaint both employers and those desiring work with the sociological reasons for the interest of the organization in furthering such a program.

In addition to encouraging an increase in part-time jobs and better utilization of workers over forty, local organizations can aid in still • other approaches to these problems. Among those proposed by the National Manpower Council are: to expand the support of scholarship and fellowship programs for young women of high ability, to increase occupational guidance for mature women, and to establish more adequate facilities to meet the needs of mature women seeking work.[19] One woman's organization which has for some time done effective work in providing financial assistance to able young women scholars is the American Association of University Women. Their aid is given both to young American women of exceptionally high promise and to young women from foreign countries wishing to study in the United States.

In the matter of establishing more adequate training programs for mature women, employers could be encouraged to make more on-the-job training or apprenticeships available. The colleges are beginning to do their part in retraining mature women. We have already described the rapidly expanding educational programs for refreshing the skills of these women, and pointed out the roles of extension divisions, junior colleges, and mass media in providing refresher education.

These are all either actual developments or proposals which suggest possible directions to be followed by local groups interested in promoting opportunities for women to live better integrated lives through continued social usefulness.

[19] National Manpower Council, *op. cit.*, pp. 3–6.

CHAPTER 10

Life Patterns in Other Countries

There is a general belief in the appearance of new forms of culture which transcend the frontiers of closed human groups.

P. CHOMBART DE LAUWE*

In many of the new countries, women want to have the status of American women, not that of their own men. Where American women succeed, others can hope that they, too, will be successful. But where they see us fail, either in the perennial tasks of women as homemakers or in the exercise of the freedom of which we have made too little use, the hands of the clock are set back for them.

MARGARET MEAD†

In the process of focusing somewhat narrowly upon personal and national aspects of our subject, let us not forget that these changes in women's status reach far beyond our national boundaries to international frontiers. They are part of a world-wide revolution. In the older countries of Europe similar transformations are occurring in women's lives, and in the newly emerging nations women's emancipation is progressing with marked rapidity. It seems appropriate to ask, what will be the American woman's contribution to the development of a fuller realization of the feminine potential?

* From P. Chombart De Lauwe, *Introduction* to "Images of Women in Society." *International Social Science Journal*, XIV, No. 1 (Paris: UNESCO, 1962), p. 19.

† From Margaret Mead, in *American Women*. The Report of the President's Commission on the Status of Women. *Prologue*. (New York: Charles Scribner's Sons, 1965), p. 6.

We have already observed the fortunate fact that coincident with the emergence of the American woman's need for broader participation is the urgency for trained womanpower in this country. America needs its womanpower, and the American woman needs to be needed. The value of women's potential for our national economy is readily apparent, but there are even more basic considerations which might be mentioned here. Today, we are returning to an emphasis upon those human qualities which built this nation. We are witnessing a revived recognition of the fact that a nation's most precious resource is its people, that our strength and safety depend upon the development of our total intellectual potentialities, our skills, and our creativeness.

One of the initial thrusts toward awakening public awareness to these values was made by the National Manpower Council, meeting at Columbia University in 1957, in an appeal to national interest concerning the waste of resources among capable American women, especially those middle-aged and older. In this connection, the Council declared that the individual's "capacity for development is still an open frontier which we have only begun to explore," and that the exploration of this capacity, "undertaken with the vigor and imagination it deserves, could initiate a new era in our national history."[1]

The higher regard for the value of womanpower as a critical resource has, of course, grown in large measure out of the pressures of the "cold war." Shortages of trained workers constitute a threat to our national security. Government spending for national defense has created many jobs of all kinds and more employment opportunities for women even in the traditionally men's fields — for instance, in electronics and engineering, as well as in teaching and public health.

But there are other reasons in the appeal for fuller utilization of womanpower aside from those of national security — reasons of an economic and social nature — which are just as urgent and, in the long run, more constructive. Among these are the need for increased productivity to support a growing population on a steadily rising standard of living; the demand for a new type of highly trained personnel, brought about by scientific and technological advancement; and the expansion and improvement of all educational and health services, not only as a result of increased population, but out of concern for national welfare. Whether through paid or voluntary employment, the

[1] National Manpower Council, *Womanpower* (New York: Columbia University Press, 1957), pp. 7–8.

chance to help in the advancement of this great national enterprise becomes a privilege for the American woman; to choose where she can best serve becomes an obligation.

But today, the responsibilities of American women do not end at national boundaries. We must assume leadership in creating for the women of underdeveloped countries an image of the emancipated woman in community relatedness. This obligation rests upon women of all countries in which rights and privileged status have been longer established.

That women of politically advanced countries have such an international role to play becomes apparent as the women of Asia and Africa are just now gaining rights that were won by American women shortly before and after the turn of the century. It is significant that, in spite of the wide differences among various countries in stages of social and economic development and in ways in which problems of women's status must be approached, the principles involved are basically the same. The differences are mainly in urgency of solutions and degrees of attainment. Thus, there exists a basis for understanding among women of various nationalities upon which programs of mutual assistance can be built.

The British experience, for instance, closely parallels our own. Faced with the problems of maintaining economic growth with a limited labor supply, economists look to married women as the principal remaining reserve. Concurrent with this national need, as in our own country, women are entering paid employment in ever-increasing numbers, the largest proportion being in the age groups between forty and sixty. The British Ministry of Labour forecasts that more than 36 per cent of all married women will be in the labor force by 1972 compared with 33 per cent in 1962. Some authorities predict an even higher increase within the decade. And Viola Klein, in her study of the British situation, found that the proportion of gainfully employed among women college graduates was considerably higher than in the general population. She comments as follows: "The employment of married women in trade and in industry, in the public services, and the professions has become part of the fabric of western life. There can be little doubt that it is as characteristic a feature of it as are an expanding economy and a rising standard of consumption, and that it is likely to last as long as these continue."[2]

[2] Viola Klein, *Britain's Married Women Workers* (London: Routledge and Kegan Paul, 1965), p. 21.

Because the employment of women on such a large scale is a relatively new phenomenon in all industrialized countries, many social and economic questions arise requiring professional research. British women appear to work for much the same reasons as those in this country. The effects upon their families are still largely to be determined, and there is concern in England as in the United States that due consideration be given to social values, that the welfare of families not be sacrificed to the economic goals of national prosperity and higher standards of living. Some research on these problems has already begun in this country and in Sweden. In England also the combination of careers and marriage and the maintenance of intellectual interests by homemakers throughout the child-rearing period have, as in this country, become of vital concern.

Other factors in the British experience, beside the national need for more workers and the increase in the numbers of women in paid employment, parallel our own situation. There is speculation about the future effects of accelerating automation upon the status of job opportunities, and concern that women may not avail themselves of the necessary education to qualify for high-ranking positions, thus retarding progress in equality of opportunities. Another vital question in both countries is whether employers are willing to make the concessions in scheduling and part-time work necessary to retain married women in paid employment. In the United States the President's Commission on the Status of Women has urged the creation of more part-time jobs for women. Viola Klein reports that in England, part-time workers are generally unpopular with management in that they are believed to be less reliable, and that employing them makes it difficult to maintain continuity of operation. Then too, training of double work-shifts and paying double insurance coverages make such arrangements expensive. She comments further that a longer period of full employment and industrial expansion will probably be required before management begins to regard married women as a "substantial and useful" part of the work force; moreover, that most employers have yet to recognize that mature women, who create a demand for part-time employment, bring to the job commendable qualities such as "regular work habits, loyalty, conscientiousness, a steadying influence, and special skills."[3]

In Sweden, another socially mature country in which women's right

[3] *Ibid.*

to gainful employment is now fully established, most problems evolving from this new pattern bear close resemblance to those in England and the United States. Public debate centers around whether and how working women are to have pay and opportunities equal to men's, and whether and how their right to work may be more fully realized in conjunction with their domestic responsibilities. Swedish sociologists are also interested in (1) the chances of marital stability in situations in which the prestige of the wife's job equals that of her husband's, and (2) the need for a more adequate system of day care centers for children.[4]

Meanwhile, the spread of urbanization and industrialization and the world-wide freeing of women from former constraints constitute a combination of phenomena which will eventually bring women of emerging nations face to face with the changes in life patterns which are now occurring among women of western cultures. In fact, in contrast to the American experience, the emancipation of women in the new and developing nations is often occurring simultaneously with industrialization. Consequently, all stages of advancement toward women's equality will probably not correspond with those in the history of the politically mature nations, and progress may be much more rapid.

In so brief a discussion we can do little more than name some of the developments which are effecting rapid change in status for women in eastern cultures. Mrs. Katie Louchheim, our Deputy Assistant Secretary for Public Affairs, points out that the reasons for the changing status of women in these regions are many and complex. Political leaders are coming to realize that advancement of the female population is an important factor in the development of their country's resources — that trained womanpower, as well as trained manpower, is essential to national progress. For male leaders who have had the opportunity to visit more advanced nations and to make comparisons, improvement in the status of their country's female population becomes a matter of pride. The fact that the young educated men are becoming bored with ignorant wives also provides a spur to the cause of women's education. Mrs. Louchheim observes incidentally that recently our own "horizons have been widened a thousandfold" as young American women are transplanted for a period in foreign lands.

---

[4] Murray Gendell, *Swedish Working Wives*. Doctoral dissertation, Dept. of Political Science, Columbia University (Totowa, New Jersey: The Bedminster Press, 1963), p. 215.

And now that they are living and working all over the world, they put their skills to work in their new surroundings — helping in a clinic or hospital, teaching in a local school, or organizing a service club. This mingling of cultures is a very important contributing factor to the rate of change.[5]

The status of women in underdeveloped countries is being advanced by preventative and curative medicines, which are beginning to lift a tremendous load from the female population in the case of the sick and the aged; and the prospects for the wider development and use of contraceptives promise to free women for the first time in history from the continuous confinements of pregnancy and infant care. Moreover, the lengthening of the life span through improved health services and better nutrition will eventually affect life patterns. Improved communications and the trend toward urban living foster the exchange of ideas and the establishment of new patterns of living, while the growth of cities and industrialization also promote education and open many new job opportunities, numbers of which will be attractive to women.

A measure of the world-wide gains in the status of women is the recent remarkable progress in granting political rights. At the close of World War II women had the right to vote and hold office in only half of the sovereign states of the world, whereas in February 1965, one hundred and six of the countries of the United Nations system granted these rights, and only six denied to women those rights possessed by men.[6] In many of the states where the franchise has been recently granted we can recognize a repetition of the stages in the evolution of our own emancipation movement. With education comes the demand for equal rights; with urbanization a demand for a larger share in paid employment opportunities; with improved public health, as seen dramatically in Japan,* the lengthening of the life

---

* Today in Japan, the older men and women appear to have aged quickly after entering their forties. However, because of advances in hygiene and public health services, those now entering their forties appear much younger. During the last thirty years the life expectancy for Japan as a whole has risen from about 43 for women and 42 for men to 68 for women and 64 for men. From R. K. Beardsley, J. W. Hall, and R. E. Ward, *Village Japan* (The University of Chicago Press, 1959), pp. 337–338.

[5] Katie Louchheim, "The Contribution of Women in a Changing World," *Department of State Bulletin,* XLVIII (May, 1963), p. 801.

[6] *Progress of Women around the World.* Pamphlet. (Washington, D.C.: U.S. Women's Bureau, February, 1965).

span, which in turn may ultimately raise the question of what to do with the increased leisure of the later years. Thus far, in the newly developing nations we find the liberals largely concerned with those issues which first absorbed the interest of American women — securing and guaranteeing rights and status.

Now we in this country, who have earlier gained so much in these respects, have before us a very specific task of constructive international leadership — to develop a philosophy of which we will make a practical application concerning the uses to be made of the rights which we have won. Educating women the world over in the meaning of their rights and the uses to be made of them is now the great concern of the United Nations Commission on the Status of Women and the agencies with which its work is closely coordinated. Through this organization there is hope of bringing to further fruition the efforts of the past half century to advance the welfare and status of the women of the world.

The work now being done by the U.N. Commission is an outgrowth of efforts which preceded it. One of the earliest international agreements was made at the Hague in 1902, dealing with conflicts in international laws governing marriage, divorce, and guardianship of children. In 1919, the Covenant of the League of Nations included articles urging humane working conditions for all, regardless of sex or age, and the suspension of traffic in women. It also set a precedent in opening the League Secretarist to women. Later, the League began work through surveys to gain detailed information on national laws concerning the status of women in the various countries of the world. However, this work was interrupted by World War II. During this early organizational period, the work of the League on behalf of women was furthered by the cooperation of the Regional Organization of American Republics, which finally at its Sixth International Conference in 1948, arrived at two inter-American agreements, granting both civil and political rights to women. These are some of the earlier efforts which form the foundations upon which the United Nations has been able to build, and which enabled the authors of the United Nations Charter to write of affirming "faith in fundamental human rights, in the dignity and worth of the human person, *in the equal rights of men and women . . .*"[7]

[7] "The United Nations and the Status of Women," Part I, *United Nations Review,* VIII, No. 3 (March 1961), 22–27.

But the rapidity with which women of the world have been given civil, political, and educational rights in the two decades since World War II can be largely accredited to the work of the United Nations in cooperation with numerous voluntary organizations. (Today, well over 300 organizations representing some phase of women's interests have consultative status with the United Nations.) A resolution urging the granting of full political rights to women was first adopted by the General Assembly of the United Nations in 1946, and two years later the Assembly proclaimed the Universal Declaration of Human Rights. Article XXI of this document declares the right of everyone "to take part in the government of his country, directly or through freely chosen representatives," as well as the right of everyone to "equal access to public service in his country."

Lacking law enforcement authority to bring about desired changes within its member nations, the United Nations Commission on the Status of Women and its parent organization, the Economic and Social Council, have succeeded in bringing about reforms by exerting pressure through public opinion. This has been done by making repeated recommendations to governments, through annual reports to the United Nations by the Secretary-General on progress toward granting women's rights within the various countries, and by international treaties. In 1952, the General Assembly adopted the United Nations' Covenant on the Political Rights of Women, an effort toward granting and protecting the rights of women on a world-wide basis. The rapid succession of states granting rights in the past two decades is largely the result of the pressures exerted through such procedures.

The many-faceted concern of the Commission is with the whole subject of family law, opportunities for occupational and professional employment, equal pay for equal work, adequate maternity leave and allowance, and part-time work for mothers whose children are in school and for older women. With the freeing of women from traditional constraints, the task of providing education, both general and vocational, takes on enormous proportions, especially in newly emerging nations. Without education, rights have little meaning, for women are not equipped to avail themselves of expanding opportunities.

Another significant part of the Commission's work is in guiding and influencing people's opinion toward wider knowledge of economic opportunities for girls and women, in order that greater participation of women in the life of the community may be made possible. But now, as political and educational rights are gradually won, another task of even greater proportions emerges. It is that of teaching the *meaning of these rights and what they imply for women as persons and as citizens.* Understanding this meaning constitutes the central task for women of all nations.

The recognition of this fact and that women of different nationalities have much to gain from sharing experience and outlooks were factors in the adoption by the General Assembly in 1956 of a plan for technical assistance in the field of the human rights, known under the title of Advisory Services in the Field of Human Rights. Under the provisions of this plan seminars were held at Bangkok, Thailand, in August 1957 for women of Asia and the Far East; at Bogota, Columbia, in May 1959 for the women of the Western Hemisphere; at Addis Ababa, Ethiopia, in December 1960, for the women of Africa. At each of these, regional conditions affecting the more active participation of women in public and civic life were discussed, including education, economic and health conditions, social and religious attitudes, and the general state of community progress. The fourth and final seminar of this series held at Lomé, Togo, in West Africa in 1963 dealt with the status of women in family law. In summarizing the results of these seminars, United Nations officials observed that:

> The success of the seminar program demonstrated that women everywhere are eager to work not only for their own advancement but for the improvement of the society in which they live. . . . By a sharing of views it is found that many problems which have been seen only in a national context, have a regional, if not a worldwide application, and it becomes apparent that these problems might be capable of solution. This lesson of hope may indeed be called the most important result achieved.
> . . . In this work, the United Nations acts at the international level to encourage and to supplement the efforts of governments and organizations, *but the goal of full equality will be reached only with the faith, encouragement and cooperation of men and women everywhere.*[8] [Italics added.]

These United Nations efforts have provided inspiration for plans to promote closer cooperation between African and American women. In April 1961 the Agency for International Development of the U.S. Department of State sponsored two ten-day regional workshops for

[8] "The United Nations and the Status of Women," Part II, *United Nations Review*, VIII, No. 4 (April 1961), 26–32.

African women educators, one at Royal University College in Nairobi, Kenya, and one at University College, Ibadan, Nigeria. These were attended by thirty-seven African women educators from fourteen countries and three regions of West and East Africa, and a delegation of American women educators. The African Regional Office offered to finance these workshops because the needs of African women seemed acute and the requests for aid were increasing so rapidly. This part of the program was followed by a study-tour by a group of African women educators to the United States. These programs are intended to become part of a continuing project. Certainly, they are evidence of the lengthening reach of American women's influence. Of the personal evaluations from the African delegates received at the close of the workshop program this one is typical: "It has made me realize that basic problems of women's and girls' education are common to all countries represented. It has enabled me to look at the problems of my own country in better perspective."[9]

As Americans, we must cultivate awareness of both the basic centrality in women's problems the world over and the local cultural differences coloring these underlying issues. The present African scene provides a striking picture of the need for such dual understanding. The rapidity of the modernization process on that continent is telescoping into a few decades many of the changes which in this country occurred during the century and a half after the Industrial Revolution. As tribal warfare is abolished and trade, western-style education, and some of our values become part of the culture, transformations are occurring in the life patterns of both men and women, as well as in the relationship of the sexes. Recent reports from Rhodesia indicate that the custom of polygamy in that country is being condemned by the ever-increasing number of educated women.[10] At the same time, there is a growing recognition of the influence of the home in training youth for a constructive role in a changing society, and of the obligations of the wife as her husband's helpmate in instances where the husband has a position of influence. Political leaders are beginning to recognize the importance of the female vote. Educational oppor-

[9] Verna C. Carley, in *Africa Women Educators Project* (Washington, D.C.: Agency for International Development, Department of State, 1962), pp. 1–23.

[10] Marie-Helene Lefaucheux, "The Contribution of Women to Economic and Social Development of African Countries," *International Labour Review*, LXXXVI (July 1962), pp. 15–20.

tunities are becoming more numerous, with a consequent tendency to postpone the marriage age and open new opportunities for women.[11] As these changes are accelerated, the problems of self-fulfillment for the educated African woman will eventually further parallel those of the American woman.

It is, of course, impossible to make broad generalizations about the status of African women, because cultural patterns are changing at varying rates in different parts of that continent. In Algeria, for instance, women have greatly hastened their own emancipation by the admiration they evoked through their bravery in the war of liberation. As a result, Algerians are more favorable toward granting rights to women, and today several women sit in the Algerian National Assembly. On the other hand, in much of tropical Africa, where brides are often purchased and afterward regarded as property by the husband's family, women's status appears to be very low according to Western standards.[12]

African women find occupational employment in towns as did American women in the late nineteenth century. In the towns they can find personal freedom and jobs which are not available to them in the villages. And here it is important to distinguish between the vast majority of women in African rural communities for whom living is primitive and burdensome, and the relatively few in the more industrialized urban centers who have achieved some degree of economic independence. A small beginning is being made in entrance to the liberal professions, with a few women as doctors, dentists, chemists, and lawyers. "Mammy traders," school teachers, nurses, hairdressers and seamstresses, typists, telephonists, and book-keepers are found in the towns. Here also are programs of adult education conducted on different levels to suit varying backgrounds, as well as voluntary women's organizations dedicated to personal advancement or community service. In Nigeria, Ghana, and Sierra Leone such clubs have now formed national councils or federations.[13]

In many respects, the interests and efforts of the better educated African women parallel those which characterized the beginnings of

[11] Adelaide C. Hill, in *Africa and the United States, Images and Realities.* Eighth National Conference, U.S. National Commission for UNESCO (Boston: Department of State Publication, 1961), p. 83.

[12] G. Mennen Williams, "Women in the New Africa," *Department of State Bulletin,* XLIX (October 21, 1963), pp. 638–9.

[13] Adelaide C. Hill, *op. cit.,* p. 83.

the women's revolution in our country. Their immediate concern is with gaining emancipation, education, and personal security, also with many legal, social, and economic problems peculiar to the particular stage of the nation's cultural development. Many of the women's groups are making a practical contribution to improving living conditions for the increasing number of single girls and women who come to the towns to seek work. Another similarity is women's stress on remaining politically active in order to preserve their rights, which in their case came as a by-product of national independence won from European domination. African women, as did those in this country, recognize that political rights are fundamental to gaining all others.

Although the educated and politically concerned among Africa's women are found mainly in isolated groups in urban areas and represent only a small percentage of the women, the existence of such groups in all the newly emergent countries holds much promise for the future. The publications of UNESCO tell us that in the more highly organized areas African women, as those in America, are beginning to look beyond their local interests to larger objectives for the enrichment of their role in society. Within a recent eighteen- month period several women's conferences have discussed many of these broader issues, those which have become the concern of educated women everywhere — health and family, expanding vocational opportunities for women, responsibilities of women in maintaining the vitality of their national culture. In August 1960, women's societies in Nigeria, assisted by the International Alliance of Women and UNESCO organized a seminar around the theme, "The African Woman Designs Her Future." Again in December of that year, the United Nations Seminar on "Challenge to African Women" was held in Addis Ababa, a gathering attended by one hundred women from thirty-one countries and territories. Regarding the African scene, the United States National Commission for UNESCO comments:

> The number of women playing an effective role in modern society is still small, of course, for the great majority remain unorganized and unrepresented. Nevertheless, the strong contributions of women to traditional society, the many important battles for emancipation won, and the apparent desire of the great majority to contribute to national development will suggest that the African women will not lag behind in the general advance of women throughout the world.[14]

[14] *Ibid.*, pp. 83–91.

As with African women, those of India gained their political rights in their nation's struggle for freedom from imperial control. In 1931, a resolution was passed by the Indian National Congress giving them the fundamental rights now embodied in the Indian Constitution. At the bidding of Ghandi, the Indian women had come out of the shelter of their homes to play a very active part in the Indian national revolution. Today, a few of the educated ones hold positions of influence both in the national and foreign services. Mrs. Indira Ghandi, India's prime minister, is representative of this relatively small number of the highly educated. In proportion to the whole population the numbers of those who are politically active are still small, but in relation to the numbers educated the ratio is high. We should also know that the demand for education among India's women is greater than the state has thus far been able to meet. This dynamic change in the position of women in India has occurred within the twentieth century and more especially within the past two decades. However, we must remember that the literacy rate for Indian women is under 10 per cent, compared with 95 per cent in some advanced countries.[15] The words of the late Prime Minister Nehru, which parallel those spoken by Dag Hammarskjold (Chapter 2), emphasize the measure of impact women's emancipation is having upon that country: "We talk of revolutions, political and economic. And yet, the greatest revolution in a country is the one that affects the status and living conditions of its women."[16]

But of special interest to us here is the broadened outlook of educated Indian women. They have indeed responded in measuring up to the responsibilities that come with political power and privilege and the opening to them of educational opportunities. They are looking beyond the narrow confines of their homes to public service. Women are found today in the legislative and administrative departments of government, in the various government services, in professions and vocations. Who, only two decades ago, would have foretold that a woman would hold the position Mrs. Ghandi holds today? With the spread of education, more and more women are dedicating themselves to the service of the people. Realizing their country's need, they

[15] *1957 Seminar on the Civic Responsibilities and Increased Participation of Asian Women in Public Life* (New York: United Nations, 1957), p. 21.

[16] Tara Ali Baig, *Women of India* (Glasgow: Publications Division, Ministry of Publication and Broadcasting, 1957), Foreword by Jawaharlal Nehru, p. V.

have enthusiastically contributed to support of the national plan for cottage industries and the newly organized Family Welfare Service, which provides medical aid, family counseling, and child care. In fact, reports indicate that India's educated women today "have gone far beyond the problems relating to their personal rights. . . . They are turning to other momentous problems. These concern the health of the people, care and protection of the backward and the indigent, the eradication of social vice, the upgrading of the underprivileged, and the preservation of India's cultural heritage."[17] Today, added to these causes, is that of limiting population increase through procedures for birth control.

In recent years, there has been considerable improvement in the employment status of Indian women, especially of those in the literate middle-classes, the largest employment rate occurring among the lower middle-class. There are now women in public life at all levels, and they are finding positions as teachers, nurses, radio officials, social service and community assistants, and clerical workers. A more favorable attitude toward women's participation in economic activity is noticeable, and it appears that with the progress of industrialization and the consequent cultural changes, the relative participation of women in the labor force will increase and occupations in which they engage become more varied.[18]

Nor are these rapid changes confined to Asia and Africa. The women of Latin America are no longer unaffected, as they have been in their past, by the political, social, and economic changes in their countries. They also are becoming keenly aware of the secondary role they have played heretofore, and are feeling the challenge to active participation in public affairs which affect their homes and their nation.[19]

All of us have heard much discussion about the status of Russian women. Their professional attainments appear to be impressive, and there seems to be no doubt that Russia values more and makes greater direct economic use of its womanpower than other countries. The largest single area of women's employment is reported to be in industry and construction, with education and health services being second, followed by transport and communications. Women are known

[17] *Ibid.*

[18] *Women in Employment,* Simla Labour Bureau, Ministry of Labour and Employment, Government of India, 1964.

[19] Joseph S. Farland, "A New Birth of Freedom," *Department of State Bulletin,* XLV (July 10, 1961), pp. 75–83.

to have taken their place, on a large scale, in many of the traditionally masculine professions and occupations — medicine, law, economics, engineering, agronomy, to mention a few, and in management and supervision at all levels. Women are reported to make up 36 per cent of all scientific personnel, as well as taking a large part in promoting cultural interests. They account for 53.7 per cent of the staff in publishing houses and editorial offices, 79.8 per cent in the book trade, 72 per cent in museums, and 96 per cent in libraries.[20]

But among the various criteria used in studying the status of women in the Soviet Union, one must take account of the basic differences in values in that country and in our own. While here and in most other countries the emancipation of women has been first interpreted as her right to vote, in Russia a woman's freedom from economic dependence on any man and her right to earn an individual wage are the basic premises. David R. Mace, speaking of these differences in values, writes: "Another principle of Soviet policy enters the picture here. The Western mind regards the creche, if not the kindergarten, as a regrettable necessity. The Soviet mind regards these institutions as a desirable commitment to the collective way of life which is essential for the smooth running of a socialist society. . . . To the Soviets, therefore, the fact that mothers are employed need involve no conflict for anyone."[21]

There is, of course, a great difference between Russian standards of living and our own. Life is hard and burdensome for Russian women. Homes and apartments are miserably overcrowded, and possessions are meager. All too often a whole family — parents, grandparents, and children — live in one room, sharing a common bathroom and kitchen with other families.[22] Centers for child care provided by the state and by industries free the Russian woman from much of her responsibility for her offspring, so that we may well raise the question concerning the price paid in family life and the welfare of the younger generation.

Moreover, the Russian woman's freedom of occupational choice is restricted, with consequent narrowing of the opportunities for self-development which would free her for creativity and the opportunity

[20] N. Tatarinova and E. Korshunova, "Living and Working Conditions of Women in the USSR," *International Labour Review*, LXXXII, No. 4 (October 1960), pp. 341–357.

[21] David R. Mace, "The Employed Mother in the USSR," *Marriage and Family Living*, XXIII (November 1961), pp. 330–331.

[22] Olga Carlisle, "The Russian Woman: Her Amazing Success and Unfulfilled Yearnings," *Saturday Evening Post*, CCXXXVIII (June 19, 1965), pp. 28–38+.

to make the particular sort of social contribution of which she is most capable. Opportunities for professional training are available specifically for those occupations where at any given time the state needs personnel. A report made by a group of foremost American educators visiting Russia in 1958 is most enlightening on this point. They note the high efficiency of the Russian educational system in achieving the strictly utilitarian results of training workers to fit the specific and immediate needs of the state. But they also emphasize the fact that, to achieve this end, what is called higher education is in fact *training* and *not education*.[23] Doubtless, because of the lack of a truly liberal approach, which we in this country prize so highly, many individual talents are never discovered or developed. Over and above the unfortunate consequences to the individuals, we may well ask whether in the long run such limitations on personal development are not extremely wasteful of the nation's human resources.

Although the American woman continues to share the goals which are now the concern of those in countries where the women's movement is of more recent origin, she has now advanced to a stage in her cultural development where her basic problem is of a different nature. It is not that of training herself in a professional specialty for the exclusive purpose of fitting into a niche selected by the state to suit its momentary needs. It is no longer in any large measure a matter of securing rights which guarantee personal security and political representation as it is now for those in newer nations. Neither is it that of opening the way to enter institutions of higher learning and the professions. Of course, it is necessary to exercise continued vigilance over these rights which have been won. But the American woman's basic problem is one which sooner or later will be encountered by those in all countries where these freedoms have been secured. It is one growing out of and transcending all these others — *of selecting from her great abundance of opportunities the direction of participation suited to her special aptitudes, of integrating her choices, and of making constructive use of the freedoms that have been won.* This goal makes higher demands upon her as an individual. It is in meeting this challenge that American women can exercise international leadership in women's affairs.

[23] *Report on Higher Education in the Soviet Union* (Pittsburgh: University of Pittsburgh Press, 1958).

Selected Bibliography

BOOKS

American Women. Report of the President's Commission on the Status of Women. New York: Charles Scribner's Sons, 1965.

BAIG, TARA ALI. *Women of India.* With Foreword by Jawaharlel Nehru. Glasgow: Publications Division, Ministry of Information and Broadcasting, 1959.

BASCOM, W. R., and HERSKOVITS, M. J. (ed.). *Continuity and Change in African Cultures:* "Changing Economic Position of Women among the Alipko Ibo." Chicago: University of Chicago Press, 1959.

BOWLBY, JOHN. *Child Care and the Growth of Love.* London: Pelican Books, 1953.

———. *Maternal Care and Mental Health.* Geneva: World Health Organization, 1952.

BRITTAIN, VERA. *The Women at Oxford.* New York: The Macmillan Co., 1960.

CAIN, GLEN G. *Married Women in the Labor Force.* Chicago: University of Chicago Press, 1966.

CASSARA, BEVERLY BENNER (ed.). *American Women: The Changing Image.* Boston: Beacon Press, 1962.

DAHLSTROM, EDMUND (ed.). *The Changing Roles of Men and Women.* Translated by Gunilla and Steven Anderman. London: Gerald Duckworth & Co., Ltd., 1967.

DAVIS, JAMES A. *Career Decisions and Educational Plans During College.* (*Great Aspirations,* Vol. I). Chicago: National Opinion Research Center, University of Chicago, 1963.

———. *Stipends and Spouses; the Finances of American Arts and Sciences Graduate Students.* Chicago: University of Chicago Press, 1962.

DENNIS, LAWRENCE E. (ed.). *Education and a Woman's Life.* Washington, D.C.: American Council on Education, 1963.

DODGE, NORTON T. *Women in the Soviet Economy.* Baltimore: The Johns Hopkins Press, 1966.

The Education of Women: Signs for the Future. Washington, D.C.: American Council on Education, 1958.

ELLIOTT, GRACE LOUCKS. *Women after Forty — The Meaning of the Last of Life.* New York: Henry Holt & Co., 1936.

FRIEDAN, BETTY. *The Feminine Mystique.* New York: W. W. Norton & Co., 1963.

GLEAZER, EDMUND J., JR. (ed.). *Junior College Directory.* Descriptive material on 655 recognized junior colleges. Washington, D.C.: American Association of Junior Colleges, 1963.

HERZOG, ELIZABETH. *Children of Working Mothers.* Washington, D.C.: U.S. Department of Health, Education, and Welfare, Children's Bureau Publication, No. 382. 1960.

JACOB, PHILIP E. *Changing Values in College.* New York: Harper & Bros., 1957.

KLEIN, VIOLA. *Britain's Married Women Workers.* The International Library of Sociology and Social Reconstruction. London: Routledge & Kegan Paul; New York: Humanities Press, 1965.

———. *Employing Married Women.* London: Institute of Personnel Management, 1961.

KOYAMA, TAKASHI. *The Changing Social Position of Women in Japan.* New York: National Agency for International Publications, 1963.

KOMAROVSKY, MIRRA. *Women in the Modern World: Their Education and Their Dilemmas.* Little, Brown & Co., 1953.

LAJEWSKI, HENRY C. *Child-Care Arrangements of Full-Time Working Mothers.* U.S. Department of Health, Education, and Welfare. Washington, D.C., 1959.

MACE, DAVID and VERA. *The Soviet Family.* New York: Doubleday & Co., 1963.

MASLOW, ABRAHAM. *Motivation and Personality.* New York: Harper & Bros., 1954.

McDONALD, EUGENE C., JR.; SMITH, BERT KRUGER; SUTHERLAND, ROBERT L. *Self-Acceptance.* Austin: The Hogg Foundation for Mental Health, 1962.

MEAD, MARGARET. *Male and Female — A Study of the Sexes in a Changing World.* New York: W. Morrow, 1949.

MUELLER, K. H. *Educating Women for a Changing World.* Minneapolis: University of Minnesota Press, 1954.

MULLER, LEO C., and MULLER, OUIDA G. (eds.). *New Horizons for College Women.* Washington, D.C.: Public Affairs Press, 1961.

MURPHY, LOIS B., and RAUSHENBUSH, ESTHER. *Achievement in the College Years.* Report on students at Sarah Lawrence College. New York: Harper & Bros., 1960.

MYRDAL, ALVA, and KLEIN, VIOLA. *Women's Two Roles: Home and Work.* London: Routledge and Kegan Paul, 1956.

NATIONAL MANPOWER COUNCIL. *Womanpower.* New York: Columbia University Press, 1957.

———. *Work in the Lives of Married Women.* New York: Columbia University Press, 1958.

NEWCOMER, MABEL. *A Century of Higher Education for American Women.* New York: Harper & Bros., 1959.

NYE, FRANCES I. and HOFFMAN, LOIS W. *The Employed Mother in America.* Chicago: Rand McNally & Co., 1963.

———. *Family Relationship and Delinquent Behavior.* New York: John Wiley, 1959.

RIESMAN, DAVID. *The Lonely Crowd: A Study of the Changing American Character.* New Haven: Yale University Press, 1950.

RICHARDSON, DOROTHY. *The Long Day: A True Story of a New York Working Girl as Told by Herself.* New York: Century Co., 1905.

SCOTT-MAXWELL, FLORIDA. *Women and Sometimes Men.* New York: Alfred A. Knopf, 1957.

SMUTS, ROBERT W. *Women and Work in America.* New York: Columbia University Press, 1959.

STRODBECK, F. L. "Family Interaction, Values, and Achievement," in D. C. McClelland, et al. *Talent and Society.* Princeton, New Jersey: Van Nostrand, 1959.

SYSIHARJU, ANNA LIISA. *Equality, Home, and Work — A Socio-Psychological Study on Finnish Student Women's Attitudes Toward Women's Role in Society.* Doctoral thesis. Helsinki: University of Helsinki, 1960.

VANVORST, BESSIE and MRS. JOHN. *The Woman Who Toils: Being the Experiences of Two Gentlewomen as Factory Girls.* New York: Doubleday, Page and Co., 1903.

WARD, BARBARA (ed.). *Women in the New Asia.* Paris: UNESCO, 1963.

WHITING, BEATRICE B. (ed.). *Six Cultures: Studies in Child Rearing.* New York: John Wiley and Sons, Inc., 1963.

WOODY, THOMAS. *A History of Women's Education in the United States.* 2 vols. New York: The Science Press, 1929.

ZAPOLEON, MARGUERITE. *Girls and Their Futures.* Chicago: Science Research Associates, 1963.

———. *Occupational Planning for Women.* New York: Harper & Bros., 1960.

ZIMAND, SAVEL (ed.). *Public Health and Welfare — The Citizens' Responsibility.* Selected papers of Homer Folks. New York: Macmillan Co., 1958.

YARROW, MARION RADKE. "Changes in Family Functioning as Intermediary Effects of Maternal Employment," in Alberta Siegel (ed.). *Research Issues Related to the Effects of Maternal Employment on Children.* University Park, Penn.: Science Research Center, 1961.

ZISSIS, CECELIA. *The Relationship of Selected Variables to the Career-Marriage Plans of University Freshmen Women.* Ann Arbor: University of Michigan, 1962.

PERIODICALS

AXELSON, LELAND J. "The Marital Adjustment and Marital Role Definitions of Husbands of Working and Non-Working Wives," *Marriage and Family Living,* XXV, No. 2 (May, 1963), 189–195.

BLOOD, ROBERT and HAMBLIN, ROBERT. "The Effect of the Wife's Employment on the Family Power Structure," *Social Forces,* XXXII (May, 1958), 347–353.

BROWN, DANIEL G. "Sex-Role Development in a Changing Culture," *Psychological Bulletin,* LIV (July, 1958), 232–242.

BUNTING, MARY I.; RAUSHENBUSH, ESTHER; and SENDERS, VIRGINIA. "Unfinished Business — Continuing Education for Women," *Educational Record,* XLII (October, 1961), 261–286.

BURIE, OLIVERA. "Images of Women in Society: Yugoslavia," *International Social Science Journal* (UNESCO), XIV, No. 1 (1962), 166–177.

"Change and Choice for the College Woman," a symposium. *Journal of the American Association of University Women.* LV, No. 4, (May, 1962).

CHOMBART DE LAUWVE, M. J. "The Status of Women in French Urban Society," *International Social Science Journal* (UNESCO), XIV, No. 1 (1962), 26–66.

CUBER, JOHN F. and HARROFF, PEGGY B. "The More Total View: Relationships among Men and Women of the Upper Middle Class," *Marriage and Family Living,* XXV, No. 2 (May, 1963), 140–145.

DAEDALUS. Journal of the American Academy of Arts and Sciences. "The Woman in America." XCIII, No. 2. Spring 1964.

DAVID, OPAL D. "A Little Discontent Becomes You," *Wellesley Alumnae Magazine,* Wellesley, Mass. (January, 1960).

———. "Factors Influencing Women's Decisions about Higher Education," *Journal of the National Association of Women Deans and Counselors,* XXIII, No. L (October, 1959), 35–39.

DOLAN, ELEANOR and DAVIS, MARGARET. "Antinepotism Rules in American Colleges and Their Effect on the Employment of Women," *Educational Record,* XLI (October, 1960), 285–295.

FARLAND, J. S. "New Birth of Freedom," *Department of State Bulletin,* XLV (July 10, 1961), 75–83.

FORGET, NELLY and NOUACER, K. "Women and the Professions in Morocco," *International Social Science Journal* (UNESCO), XLV, No. 1 (1962), 92–130.

FULLER, FRANCES M., and BATCHELDER, MARY B. "Opportunities for Women at the Administrative Level." An Appraisal of the Radcliffe Management Training Program. *Harvard Business Review,* XXXL (January-February, 1953).

GARDNER, D. BRUCE; HAWKS, GLENN R.; and BURCHINAL, LEE G. "Noncontinuous Mothering in Infancy and Development in Later Childhood," *Child Development,* XXXII (June, 1961), 225–234.

GASS, GERTRUDE ZEMON. "Counselling Implications of Women's Changing Roles," *Personnel and Guidance Journal,* XXXVI (March, 1959), 482–487.

GETTELL, RICHARD G. "Plea for the Uncommon Woman," *School and Society,* LXXXVI (June, 1958), 259–261.

GLICK, PAUL C. "The Life Cycle of the Family," *Marriage and Family Living,* XVII, No. 1 (February, 1955), 3–9.

GLUECK, SHELDON, and GLUECK, ELEANOR. "Working Mothers and Delinquency," *Mental Hygiene,* XLI, No. 3 (July, 1957), 327–353.

GOVER, DAVID A. "Socio-Economic Differential in the Relationship between Marital Adjustment and the Wife's Employment Status," *Marriage and Family Living,* XXV, No. 4 (November, 1963), 452–458. (Including discussion by Robert O. Blood, Jr., and comment by F. Ivan Nye.)

HAHN, L. B. "U.N. Promotion of Equality for Women," *U.S. Department of State Bulletin,* XXXVIII (June 2, 1958), 930–933.

HARBESON, G. E. "Your Home and America's Future," *Journal of the American Association of University Women,* LII, No. 3 (March, 1959), 147–150.

HARTLEY, RUTH E. "Current Patterns in Sex Roles: Children's Perspectives," *Journal National Association Women Deans and Counselors,* XXV, 1 (October, 1961), 3–13.

HEER, D. M. "Dominance and the Working Wife," *Social Forces,* XXXVI (May, 1958), 341–347.

———. "Husband and Wife Perceptions of Family Power Structure." *Marriage and Family Living,* XXIV (February, 1962), 65–67.

HEIST, PAUL. "Commentary on the Motivation and Education of College Women," *Journal of the National Association of Women Deans and Counselors,* XXV (January, 1962), 51–60.

HOFFMAN, LOIS W. "Effects of the Employment of Mothers on Parental Relations and the Division of Household Tasks," *Marriage and Family Living,* XXII (February, 1960), 27–35.

"Images of Women in Society," A symposium. *International Social Science Journal* (UNESCO), XIV, No. 1 (1962).

JAHODA, MARIE, and HAVEL, JOAN. "Psychological Problems of Women in Different Social Roles," *Educational Record,* XXXVI (October, 1955), 325–326.

JOYCE, JOSEPH. (Birkbeck College, University of London), "A Research Note on Attitudes Toward Work and Marriage of Six Hundred Adolescent Girls," *British Journal Sociology,* XII, 2 (June, 1961), 176–183.

KLOSKOWSKA, A., and PIETROWSKI, J. "Images of Women in Society: Polish Working Class Families," *International Social Science Journal* (UNESCO), XIV, No. 1 (1962), 66–92.

KORNER, IJA N. "Of Values, Value Lag, and Mental Health," *The American Psychologist,* XI (October, 1956), 543–546.

LICHTENSTEIN, HYMAN, and BLOCK, H. R. "The Middle-Aged Coed in Evening College," *Adult Education,* XIII, No. 4 (Summer, 1963), 234–240.

MACE, DAVID R. "The Employed Mother in the USSR," *Marriage and Family Living* (November, 1961), pp. 330–333.

MCGHEE, G. C. "Women and the Goal of World Community," *Department of State Bulletin,* XLV (July 3, 1961), 29–32.

MONTAGUE, ASHLEY A. "Triumph and Tragedy of the American Woman," *Saturday Review,* XLI (September 27, 1958), 13–15.

NEWCOMER, MABEL. "Women's Education: Facts, Findings, and Apparent Trends," *Journal of the National Association of Women Deans and Counselors,* XXIV, No. 1 (October, 1960).

NYE, F. IVAN. "Employment Status of Mothers and Adjustment of Adolescent Children," *Marriage and Family Living,* XXI (August, 1959), 240–244.

———. "Employment Status of Mothers and Marital Conflict, Permanence, and Happiness," *Social Problems,* VI (Winter, 1959), 265–266.

———. "Maternal Employment and Marital Interaction: Some Contingent Conditions," *Social Forces,* XL, No. 2 (December, 1961), 113–119.

OLSEN, M. E. "Distribution of Family Responsibilities and Social Stratification," *Marriage and Family Living,* XXII (February, 1960), 60–65.

PETERSON, ESTHER. "Experiment in Sweden," *Women's Education,* Publication of the American Association of University Women, Washington, D.C., III, No. 2 (June, 1963).

PARRISH, JOHN B. "Professional Womanpower as a National Resource," *Quarterly Review of Economics and Business* (University of Illinois, Urbana), I (February, 1961), 54–64.

———. "Women in Top Level Teaching and Research," *AAUW Journal,* LV, No. 2 (January, 1962), 99–103.

ROCHER, G., *et al.* "Images of Women in Society: Canada, Ivory Coast, Togo," *International Social Science Journal* (UNESCO), XIV, No. 1 (1962), 130–137.

ROSE, A. M. "Factors Associated with the Life Satisfactions of Middle-Class, Middle-Aged Persons," *Marriage and Family Living,* XVII (February, 1955), 15–19.

———. "The Voluntary Association: Instrument of Change," *AAUW Journal,* LV, No. 4 (May, 1962), 266–269.

ROSENMAYR, LEOPOLD. "Images of Women in Society: The Austrian Woman," *International Social Science Journal* (UNESCO), XIV, No. 1 (1962), 157–166.

SHERRARD, EDITH H. "The Changing Volunteer in a Changing Society," *Journal of the American Association of University Women,* LV, No. 2 (January, 1962), 88–89.

SIEGAL, ALBERTA E., and Others. "Development and Independence in Children of Working Mothers," *Child Development,* XXX (December, 1959), 533–546.

STOLZ, LOIS MEEK, and Others. "Effects of Mothers' Employment on Children: Evidence from Research," *Child Development,* XXI (December, 1960), 749–782.

"The United Nations and the Status of Women," Pt. 1, *United Nations Review,* VIII, No. 3 (March, 1961), 22–27; Pt. 2, VIII, No. 4 (April, 1961), 26–32.

TOMASSON, RICHARD F. "The Swedes Do It Better," *Harper's Magazine,* CXCVIII, No. 1349 (October, 1962), 178–180.

WHITE, WINSTON. "Individual and Society: a New Perspective," *AAUW Journal,* LV, No. 4 (May, 1962), 276–283.

YARROW, MARION R., *et al.* "Child-rearing in Families of Working and Nonworking Mothers," *Sociometry,* XXV, No. 2 (June, 1962), 121–140.

———, "Maternal Deprivation: Toward an Empirical and Conceptual Reevaluation," *Psychological Bulletin,* LVIII (November, 1961), 459–490.

U.S. GOVERNMENT PUBLICATIONS

CARLEY, VERNA A. *African Women's Educators Project* (U.S. Department of State, Agency for International Development), 1962.

Employing Older Workers. (U.S. Department of Labor, Bureau of Employment Security), 1959.

Employment of Older Women. An Annotated Bibliography on Hiring Practices, Attitudes, and Work Performance. (U.S. Department of Labor, Women's Bureau), 1957.

Fifteen Years after College — A Study of Alumnae, Class of 1945. (U.S. Department of Labor, Women's Bureau), 1961.

1965 Handbook on Women Workers. (U.S. Department of Labor, Women's Bureau Bulletin 290), 1965.

HILL, ADELAIDE C. "Broadening Horizons for African Women," *Africa and the United States — Images and Realities.* (Eighth National Conference, Boston, 1961, U.S. National Commission for UNESCO. Department of State Bulletin 7332, African Series 26), 1961.

Manpower Challenge of the 1960's. (U.S. Department of Labor, Bureau of Labor Statistics), 1961.

Meet the Over-40 Worker. (U.S. Department of Labor), 1960.

Occupational Outlook Publications. Professions and Job Descriptions. (Publication of the U.S. Department of Labor, Women's Bureau).

Part-Time Employment for Women. (U.S. Department of Labor, Women's Bureau Bulletin 273), 1960.

Research in Child Welfare. (Report of a Conference in Washington, D.C., December 15 and 16, 1960. Social Security Administration, Children's Bureau Publication 389), 1961.

Today's Woman in Tomorrow's World. (Proceedings of a Conference held in June, 1960, Washington, D.C., U.S. Department of Labor, Women's Bureau Bulletin 276), 1960.

MISCELLANEOUS

BACON, DEBORAH. "Voluntary Non-Returns." An analysis and description of 351 undergraduate women at the University of Michigan who did not return at the end of the 1958–59 year. Ann Arbor: Office of the Dean of Women, 1960.

College Teaching as a Career. Washington, D.C.: American Council on Education, 1959.

DOUVAN, ELIZABETH, and KAYE, CAROL. *Study of Adolescent Girls,* Motives in planning for college among 1925 Girl Scouts. Ann Arbor: Survey Research Center, University of Michigan, 1959.

Futures for College Women in New York. Published periodically since October, 1960. New York: Alumnae Advisory Center, 541 Madison Avenue.

HALFTER, IRMA. *The Comparative Academic Achievement of Women Forty Years of Age and Over and Women Eighteen to Twenty-Five Years of Age.* Abstract of recent Ph.D. thesis at University of Chicago. The Author, Department of Psychological Testing, DePaul University, Chicago.

HARTLEY, RUTH E. *Children's Concepts of Male and Female Roles. Some Implications of Current Changes in Sex-Role Patterns; Sex-Role Patterns and the Socialization of the Male Child.* The Author, Department of Psychology, The City College, New York, N.Y.

HILL, F. F. "Education in the Developing Countries." Reprint. New York: *International Development Review,* December, 1962.

Mademoiselle Looseleaf Career File. Job descriptions and qualifications. Illustrated. New York: *Mademoiselle,* 1948 to date.

MATTHEWS, ESTHER E. *The Marriage-Career Conflict in the Career Development of Girls and Young Women.* Unpublished Ph.D. Dissertation. Cambridge, Mass.: Harvard University Library, 1960.

Minnesota Plan for the Continuing Education of Women. Leaflet. Minneapolis: Center for the Continuing Education of Women, University of Minnesota, 1961.

Radcliffe Institute for Independent Study. Prospectus explaining purpose and operations of the plan. Cambridge, Mass.: Radcliffe College, 1961.

Rutgers University. *A Program for the Retraining in Mathematics of College Graduate Women.* New Brunswick, New Jersey: Rutgers — The State University, 1961.

Sarah Lawrence College. *Work in Progress.* Study of the First-Year Activities of the Center for Continuing Education. Bronxville, New York: Sarah Lawrence College, 1963.

SCOFIELD, NANETTE E. *Some Changing Roles of Women in Suburbia.* Reprint of paper presented before the New York Academy of Sciences. Washington, D.C.: Publication Office of the American Association of University Women, 1961.

Teaching by Television. Second edition. A Report of the Ford Foundation and the Fund for the Advancement of Education. New York: The Ford Foundation, 1961.

Womanpower. Young Fabian pamphlet No. 11. London: Fabian Society, 1966.

APPENDIX

SELECTED READINGS:

INTERNATIONAL PERSPECTIVES ON WOMEN'S CHANGING LIFE PATTERNS

The Universality of Sex Role Changes*

It is an undeniable fact of recent history that almost the whole world has seen revolutionary changes in the status of women — politically, legally, economically, educationally. The formal changes are not hard to discover. In country after country during the last fifty years, women have gained the right to vote, to stand for election, to hold property in their own right, to plead their own cases at law, to enter all forms of paid employment and to seek educational qualifications on equal terms with men. That there still remain certain anomalies and inequalities which are the special concern of the United Nations Commission on the Status of Women, does not alter the general picture. It is one of revolutionary change — *de jure*. What is harder to evaluate is the meaning of the change *de facto*. What, so far, do these revolutionary formal changes amount to in practice?

The "woman question", as it was once called in England, is also the "man question". One cannot meaningfully discuss the status and role of women without discussing also — if only by implication — the status and role of the other half of the human race. — What concerns us primarily is not simply the change in the political and legal status of women, or even their advance in economic and educational opportunity as such, but the bearing of all these things, and other concomitant changes too, upon everyday living. And this must also include both sexes.

Most of us spend by far the larger part of everyday living in families, a fact which necessarily involves us closely with one another, and forces us to consider the reciprocal social roles of males and females. The kinds of family we live in are very various, and the relationships that exist between male and female members, both in personal terms

---

* Excerpts from Barbara Ward, *Women in the New Asia: the Changing Social Roles of Men and Women in South and Southeast Asia.* Paris: UNESCO, 1963. Reprinted by permission. Italics are the author's.

and as regards the division of labor, are also various. But all of this variety represents merely different methods of dealing with similar problems: problems of child-rearing, of domestic happiness, of social security. *In a time of rapid change, such as the one we all live in now, when our own views upon how best to meet these perennial and ubiquitous problems are in a state of flux, we may be helped at least toward clarity of thinking by considering some of the ways in which other peoples have been tackling them.*

Images of Women
in Society*

Never before has the social status of women raised so many questions throughout the world, and never before has it appeared so clearly that the evolution of social structures is linked up with these questions. . . . In both the East and the West, the declarations of principle, the vehement discussions in the political world, the trends of public opinion and articles in the press constitute so many proofs of the scope and importance of this problem.

It is not women's social status and the evolution of this status which form the object of our study, but the image which men and women in various parts of the world form about them according to their culture, the industrial changes that are taking place, the new trends of thought that arise, the place which they themselves occupy in the community, their own personal experience. Our aim is to understand how people perceive and represent to themselves the status of women in relation to the different social structures and how they view changes in this status. The images thus formed and their modifications can either delay or accelerate changes in the actual status of women; in some cases, they may even be real agents of change if they correspond to the deep aspirations of the peoples.

In relation to the various problems raised in all countries in connexion with the evolution of the status of women, two images deserve special attention: that of women at work and that of the equality of the sexes.

The image of women at work shows a number of instructive differences between the countries concerned. Polish workers accept much more readily than French workers the idea of women (whether married or single) going out to work, but, in the case of mothers with small

* Excerpts from P. Chombart de Lauwe, "Introduction" to *Images of Women in Society*. A symposium. *International Social Science Journal* (UNESCO), XIV, No. 1 (1962). Reprinted by permission.

children, there is almost universal opposition to this idea in both France (95 per cent) and Poland (96 per cent). In Morocco, the proportion of those opposed to this idea is much higher owing to very lively traditional images, but extremely rapid changes are taking place. In Canada, the image of woman considered exclusively as a wife and mother seems more imbedded in the very structure of the country, which is both highly developed economically and making rapid progress.

In every country, the reasons inducing women to work are chiefly of a financial nature (almost 100 per cent of those interviewed in France), but, whereas in the poorer sections of the community women work in order to subsist, in the more well-to-do sections they do so in order to earn more money for leisure, culture and amusements for themselves and their families.

The other reasons are invoked much less frequently. In general, they reveal differences of opinion between the men and women interviewed. Boredom at home and a bent for the work in question occupy a fairly small place among the reasons given in the various countries. The desire for independence was mentioned only very rarely in Morocco. Perhaps it plays a more important role in Tropical Africa. In France, this independence is the privilege of the well-to-do classes, which alone have a real freedom of choice owing to their higher standard of life. We are here touching on a fundamental question, to which we have often referred, namely the relationship between material hardship and limited aspirations. In Poland, many women would like to work, but most husbands are opposed to the idea. Most women who work would prefer to stop doing so, while many of those who do not have a job would like one. In France, we find similar differences of opinion among workers, but, owing to bad working conditions, low rates of pay and the "single wage" rule (taken in conjunction with the traditional patterns of life), women belonging to the working classes prefer to remain at home. On the other hand, women belonging to the more well-to-do sections of the community prefer to work outside the home, whatever their actual situation.

The drawbacks of women's work are stressed mainly by men. Promiscuity of the sexes and the danger of indecorous behaviour are weighty arguments in Morocco and by no means negligible in France (where the importance attached to them varies according to the different environments). The refusal to take orders from a woman is also very frequent in Morocco, but it is also to be found elsewhere. Almost everywhere, neglect of children and household duties is adduced. In general, these various objections readily produce a feeling of guilt among women even in industrialized countries.

To sum up, it may be said that most of the persons interviewed have the following "guiding image" concerning women's work: unmarried women must work (apart from the objection made in Morocco and by certain Polish workers that girls should be trained for their traditional role as wives, and the fear in certain well-to-do sections of the French population that women will acquire financial independence too easily); married women without children may work (but some men make certain reservations); married women with small children must not work, except in special cases.

The question of the equality of men and women in the family and in society arises in connexion with both work and other activities. The influence of paid employment on the equality of the sexes at home is recognized in countries where there is already a fairly high proportion of women workers, and this fact is sometimes a source of apprehension. Further, when women are employed outside the home there is frequently a tendency to insist upon equal rights in the place of employment. Work is readily regarded as a means of repairing an injustice and of giving women more "dignity" in social life.

The earning of a second wage by the wife tends everywhere to modify profoundly the traditional financial roles. In Poland and in France, the management of the family budget, which, in working families, was the wife's responsibility (more often owing to the husband's lack of interest than to deliberate domination on the part of the wife), is gradually slipping out of her control. Financial responsibilities and tasks are being shared more and more equally. In Morocco and in well-to-do sections of the French population, a similar situation is arising but more gradually and starting from a reverse situation, since wives took little or no part in financial matters.

The Polish image of women as first and foremost good housewives, then good mothers of kindly disposition has as a counterpart the image of men as fathers who must above all earn the family's money, set a good example, be attached to the home and, lastly, take an interest in the children's education. The ideas entertained by members of the French working classes are much the same, and perhaps even more traditional ideas exist in Canada. In Morocco, owing to the influence of religious doctrines, it is difficult for women to assume overt responsibilities, but it is recognized that mothers must play an essential role in education.

The persistence of these images partly explains why men, and to a large extent women too, are alarmed at the profound changes in the social hierarchy and in the social relations between the two sexes. The French and Moroccan surveys are particularly explicit in this respect. Few Polish workers seem to fear a loss of prestige in the home, but the apprehensions of the components of the French sample are more complicated. The women themselves distrust their own aggressiveness which reveals itself when they acquire their new status. The harmony between man and wife is at stake, and the possibility of true love seems to be less certain. It is here that we begin to see what happens when images and behaviour cease to coincide.

These few remarks suffice to show certain possibilities of comparison, but it is mainly on the general questions of evolution raised by such a survey of images that we must concentrate our attention. The transformation of the status of women, which accompanied the transition from traditional to industrialized societies, the perception of this evolution, the aspirations to which it gave rise, and the influence of dynamic images on planning constitute many questions.

Whatever the theory, the author or the country, the remarks made concerning the consequences of cultural exchanges reveal a wide measure of agreement. . . . There is a general belief in the appearance of new forms of culture which transcend the frontiers of closed human groups. However, the study of the emergence of the new images which inspire these changes entails certain difficulties which ought not to be overlooked.

Obviously, the image of the mother in Moroccan society can be studied only in relation to all the other cultural aspects of the same society; and this society, in its turn, must be studied in relation to all other Moslem societies. The image of woman as a worker, however, which clashes with that of woman as a mother, can be illustrated only by comparisons with more highly industrialized societies. We have thus constantly to work at several levels of comparison.

Subject to the foregoing remarks, it may be said that human behaviour and the images which determine it are closely linked with the social environments in which men live their daily lives. . . . Thus, the cultural characteristics of a particular group or of a social environment can be just as important as the cultural characteristics of a particular society. The notions of sub-culture and culture are becoming more and more relative. An image of the Frenchwoman or of the American woman is becoming increasingly rare among the inhabitants of France and America, where the image is more and more likely to vary according to the environment.

Owing to the various influences to which the persons interviewed are subjected, we devoted special attention, from the outset, to the divorce between behaviour in particular circumstances and the images which habitually determine the attitudes of the persons concerned. . . . The fundamental point is thus the rupture, confirmed by most of the reports presented, between guiding images, in which the traditional elements often predominate, and actual behaviour in particular circumstances. Thus, the Moroccan woman who goes to work may sometimes be "ashamed" to have to do so, because her guiding image is still that of the traditional mother who confines herself to home life. On the other hand, a member of the French middle classes may sincerely accept the new image of the woman worker, and at the same time feel that his own wife should remain at home owing to the particular circumstances in which he finds himself.

We have emphasized the influence of perception on the creation of guiding images, but the perception of evolution is an even more important factor than the perception of actual situations. When individuals become aware of changes that have already occurred, they also become alive to the possibility of other changes. New aspirations appear, and with them fears and misgivings. This is the fundamental aspect of the process. It is because of this perception of evolution that a woman can hope to free herself from an oppressive situation, but, at the same time, she may fear the consequences — to which we have already referred — with respect to her home life. . . . From the international survey as a whole, as well as from present-day literature, the press and the cinema, one fact emerges clearly, namely the creation of a new image of woman in society. This image gives rise to vehement controversy, for it implies not only a change in the relations between the sexes but also a transformation of the social structure as a whole.

The idea of the complete equality of the sexes is clearly gaining ground. Men and women have a feeling that it reflects the truth, but they are afraid of it, each in his or her own particular way. The right of women to vote is more readily admitted than their right to work or the possibility of their exercising authority, for such a right represents a less radical change in the traditional relations between the sexes. The revolution in progress is much more profound and much more far-reaching; thus . . . it is not surprising that it should give rise to such deep feeling. The feminist "counter-myths" which are opposed to the traditional myths of virility create a climate in which rational arguments lose some of their force. In the long run, it is in the notion of the married couple that we must seek the solution to the problem.

What good would it do man to maintain his "superiority" and what good would it do woman to gain her "freedom" if in doing so they felt themselves strangers to one another or enemies? That is why it is so important for the future that the two sexes should adopt a common guiding image. Many women have expressed the fears they experience with regard to their own aggressiveness and their desire for revenge. An ancient rivalry between the sexes is again coming to the fore. How can we set it aside today and prevent it from becoming more acute than ever? Family responsibilities are being increasingly shared, relations between the spouses are changing and improving, and equality is gradually being established on a firmer basis; but, we repeat, the differences remain and it is precisely these differences which make married life possible.

Here, we could reopen the discussion on nature and culture, but would it lead us very far? In terms of evolution, the problem presents a different aspect. Biological evolution and social evolution are not opposed to one another; in both cases, it is possible to imagine a gradual progress towards equality despite the subsistence of differences; but it is hardly possible to conceive of a gradually increasing similitude which would ultimately lead to complete solitude.

The apprehensions felt by . . . men and women . . . will not be dispelled until conditions conducive to a true emancipation of women and to a real communion between husband and wife have been established. The transformation of the social structures as a whole . . . must be inspired by the new image of woman. The organization of work must be thought out afresh. Hours of work, holidays, wage scales, social relations in the workshops, the distribution of tasks, vocational guidance, social promotion, etc., must be organized with due regard to the needs and aspirations linked up with the new image of woman. Social life in the residential areas must also be reorganized in order to enable women to be freed from numerous tasks which at present place a crushing burden on them. The equipment for social, health, cultural and particularly educational purposes must be improved. The conception of crèches, day nurseries, nursery schools, ordinary schools and youth clubs will depend on the role assigned to women. The conception of education and instruction is also closely linked up with the image of woman. The distribution of tasks between the school and the family depends to a large extent on women's role in education.

The evolution of the structures and functions of the family as we are studying it in other projects will also be influenced mainly by the conception of woman's role in society. Relations between spouses and family relationships will depend on the image of woman. Even the father's role completely changes if women assume new responsibilities. We know the importance of the image of the father's role in the evolution of social relations. The relationship between family authority and social authority has already been emphasized so often that there is no need to dwell on it here.

The importance of research on the perception of the evolution of the status of women as well as on the patterns, behaviours and guiding images associated with it will, we trust, be more evident after these brief remarks. We must, however, recall the limits of our study, which are due largely to the fact that the research in question is linked up with the evolution of all the social structures. What matters to us is that men and women in various countries should be aware of the evolution of society. . . . It is necessary . . . to link up the new image of woman in society with the images of the family of the future, of the ideal child, of the town of the future, of social classes, of the State, of religion, etc. International surveys will have to be developed with due regard to these fundamental relationships.

British Women
Look into the Future*

If the present trend [in Britain] continues, there will by 1973 be nearly nine million women in employment of whom over 60 per cent will be married. Women as a whole will, then as now, form roughly 34 per cent of the working population; but the proportion of married women, excluding widows, divorced and separated women, will have risen from 52 to 60 per cent, and is expected to rise to 62 per cent of all working women by 1980.

The Ministry of Labour, on whose published figures the above percentages are based, proceeds from the assumption that there will be full employment and that the marriage age of women will continue to fall, while the proportion of young people between the ages of 15 and 24 staying in full-time education will go on rising. It does not allow, however, for the raising of the school leaving age to sixteen on which the Government has meanwhile decided and which will further reduce the number of single women available for work from 1970/71 onwards.

According to the official estimates, more than 36 per cent of all married women will be gainfully employed by 1972, compared with 33 per cent in 1962.

The National Institute of Economic and Social Research, using the same data, but applying a different method of projection (namely, a "cohort analysis"), arrives at an even higher "participation rate": it estimates that in 1972 39.4 per cent of all married women will be at work, the largest proportion in the age groups between forty and sixty.

Within the next decade, therefore, all but two-thirds of the female working population will be married if these forecasts come true.

These estimates may, however, err on the conservative side, for they rely entirely on demographic data and allow neither for changes in

* Excerpts from Viola Klein, *British Married Women Workers.* The International Library of Sociology and Social Reconstruction. London: Routledge & Kegan Paul; New York: Humanities Press, 1965. Reprinted by permission.

the general climate of opinion nor for the influence which more and better education may have on women's attitude towards continued employment.

In a study I recently carried out among married women college graduates in this country I found that the proportion of my sample who were gainfully occupied was significantly higher than in the corresponding age groups of married women in the population as a whole. . . . It may be of interest that, excluding widows and divorced women, some 55 per cent of the graduates covered by my survey were gainfully employed in 1963, the majority in part-time jobs; this compares with roughly 42 per cent of the married women of the same age range in the general population.

A recent study has shown that in France, too, the activity rate of women is in direct relation to their educational level. Broken down by the subjects in which their qualifications were achieved, the highest proportion employed is among women with medical and social science qualifications (82.4 per cent), followed by those with arts degrees (77.4 per cent) and scientific and technical qualifications (75 per cent). This compares with an employment rate of 41.5 per cent of women without higher education.

The reasons for this tendency are easy to see. The more highly trained a woman is, the more rewarding her employment will be both intellectually and financially. Education will not only have qualified her to hold a more interesting and responsible job, but it will, more often than not, have promoted the habit of seeking satisfaction in mentally stimulating work.

Moreover, scientific, technological and economic developments of recent years have been such as to multiply the number and variety of occupations requiring a high degree of education and technical skill. The opportunities for employment are therefore best for people with the highest qualifications. There have been shortages of skilled personnel even during a period of recession and in regions of relatively high unemployment. The incentives for married women to use their professional qualifications are therefore strong. They have been accompanied in a number of professions, where shortages have been most acute — among which have been the traditionally 'feminine' occupations such as teaching, nursing and social work — by an atmosphere in which the withholding of one's service entails a moral conflict.

The proportion of professionally and technically qualified persons in the working population will continue to grow as our economic and social life gets increasingly geared to the scientific developments of our time. An American forecast of labour force requirements in 1970 estimated that the rate of growth in professional and technical occupations will be more than 40 per cent during the decade 1960–1970. This is about twice as much as for the labour force as a whole and compares, for instance, with 18 per cent in semi-skilled and 25 per cent in service occupations. The estimated growth — if this is the right word — among unskilled occupations during the same period is nil.

Corresponding projections of changes in particular occupational groups are not yet available in this country. There can, however, be little doubt that the trend will be in the same general direction as in the United States, that is, towards a disproportionate increase in professional and semi-professional occupations.

Hand in hand with the growing need for qualified personnel in industry and the professions, in State and Local Government and a variety of other services, goes a greatly increased emphasis on educational expansion. Never before has the interest in more and better education been as keen, and shared by as many people, as it is today. The desire to provide opportunities for all who are capable of benefiting from higher education now extends to women as well as men. Indeed, it has been made clear by various authorities including the Robbins Committee that the so-called "pool of ability" — that is, the hitherto unused reserve of native intelligence on which the community will have to draw if it is to make the best use of its human resources — is to be found among women to a larger extent than among men.

If it can, therefore, be expected that in future a higher percentage of women will receive a better education or vocational training than has been customary to date, it is fair to assume that a correspondingly larger proportion of them will wish to continue, or later return to, their careers after marriage.

Those who have the opportunity of interviewing women students have been struck lately by the matter-of-fact way in which the new pattern has been accepted: most of the girls entering universities now seem to expect to marry, to interrupt their careers in order to raise a family, and later to return to a professional occupation when their children are off their hands; and many girls are influenced by this anticipated pattern in their choice of a career.

For these reasons it may well be that the "activity rate" of married women — i.e. the proportion of them in gainful employment — will in future be higher than a study of past employment trends and current marriage ages might suggest.

It would become higher still if Government and the public decided actively to support this social change — which, so far, has taken place mainly by its own momentum — by making it somewhat easier for married women to discharge their domestic responsibilities while working away from home.

There are social as well as economic reasons for helping married women to carry out their dual task.

The economic reasons are the more obvious ones and are now widely understood: There can be no economic growth without an expansion of the labour force even if the productivity per worker increases. Short of importing more immigrant labour — which, even if resorted to, could hardly solve the problem in the rapidly growing sector of technical and professional occupations — there is no means of increasing the working population other than by making better use of the skills and talents of women in this country.

"The question is the more important", states the National Institute of Economic and Social Research . . . "since it seems that it is only if there is an increase in the number of married women who want to work that there will be a substantial rise in Britain's labour force in the next decade".

The National Economic Development Council has also recognized this need, and in its Report has recommended special measures, such as more part-time jobs, the arrangement of convenient shifts and working hours, the provision of vocational guidance, training and refresher courses "to make it easier for married women wishing to do so to enter employment".

Both quotations, it will be noted, refer to married women "wanting to work" or "wishing to enter employment". That is to say, the voluntary nature of their activity is underlined in each case; it is assumed, on the basis of recent experience, that many would choose to work if given the opportunity.

Because for most married women today gainful employment is optional, as opposed to the care of home and family which is compulsory, the social needs of those who voluntarily (and, by the standards of some people, "wantonly") take upon themselves an extra burden are often overlooked. Their difficulties, because they are thought to be "self-inflicted", often earn them little sympathy.

In the case of working wives, the people most concerned about the possibly harmful effects of employment on the women themselves and on their families are the same who most strongly oppose the introduction or expansion of services which might alleviate the lot of working mothers and their families. Their argument is that such services might encourage even more married women to go out to work. They fear, in other words, what the economists hope for, namely, an increase in the number of married women working. The economists themselves are anxious to avoid the onus of "encouraging" wives and mothers to take up employment. Their suggestion is merely to help those who would like to work in any case.

The fear of offering incentives for married women to seek gainful employment is due, on the one hand to the welcome recognition that important social values are involved which should not be allowed to be overridden by purely economic considerations: however desirable national prosperity and rising standards of living may be, the health and happiness of the women, their husbands and children, and the stability of the family must not be jeopardized in the pursuit of material progress.

On the other hand, the reluctance to engage married women in the economic effort of the nation during peacetime is due to uncertainty of the consequences and to fear bred of ignorance.

The employment of married women of all social classes in modern conditions of life and work is a recent phenomenon, however widespread it may be. Too recent, in fact, to have permitted the thorough scientific investigations of its psychological and social effects which alone could form the basis of a rational and balanced judgment. In their absence, opinions are based on emotional bias and preconceived ideas.

The fears concerning the physical and nervous strain on women resulting from their dual responsibilities have, by and large, proved unfounded. . . . Generally improved working conditions and the five-day week, as well as labour-saving devices in the home, have helped to make a combination of employment and housework less burdensome. It is true, of course, that apart from widows, divorced women and other cases of hardship, which fortunately are the exception rather than the rule, those women whose health does not stand up to the strain, or who "cannot cope", can give up working outside their homes. In this sense, working wives represent a selected group and it would be wrong to conclude that what is true of them applies with equal force to all women.

However, one-in-three is a sufficiently large proportion of married women to allow the generalization that for many of them the compensations of employment away from home carry sufficient weight to offset the additional work and strain involved. Indeed, it is not uncommon for doctors to recommend their women patients to take a job as a remedy for "housewives' neurosis". It certainly is one way out of the social isolation from which so many urban and suburban housewives today suffer.

Work outside their homes has moreover . . . helped to restore to women their sense of usefulness, which had suffered by the reduction of domestic functions, and has consequently renewed their self-confidence. They have come to feel that they are needed in the home as well as by the community: as women and as workers.

Husbands . . . have adjusted themselves to the new situation better than might have been expected. Marriage is more popular than it has ever been before and has, indeed, been made easier by the fact that young women carry on in their jobs, at least for some time, to contribute to the capital outlay involved in setting up a new home.

The main uncertainty and anxiety in relation to married women's employment which still remain, therefore concern the effect of their partial withdrawal from home on their children.

This is a field in which we still mostly grope in the dark. In large part, our ignorance is due to the complexity of the problem which defies any simple analysis of cause and effect. Partly, however, it appears to be due to an inexplicable lack of interest.

Nobody knows, for instance, how many mothers of young children go out to work, nor how many children, and of what ages, are affected.

Statistically it would be possible that one-third — and even as many as one-half — of all married women might be employed without involving a single child: so many households without children under the age of 16 are there in the country.

In practice, however, as anyone knows from observation, this is not true; among the working wives there is a proportion of mothers of young children — but how large this proportion is appears to be nobody's business to find out.

This is the kind of factual information which could fairly easily be obtained by simple survey techniques — and which is available in some other countries.

Of much greater complexity is the question of the possible psychological effects on children of their mothers going out to work. The question is so difficult to answer because the factor "maternal employment" cannot with any degree of certainty be disentangled from other elements of the situation with which it is closely interwoven. The widespread employment of women outside the home is part of a much wider stream of social change from which it cannot be isolated. Among the many influences which make themselves felt in the formation of a character — who could honestly venture to put his finger on a spot and say: these personality traits are due to social mobility; those to the competitiveness of our culture; those to its prosperity; those to the impact of mass media; or to a philosophy of individualism and self-reliance (to name but a few of the components of the contemporary social climate) — and these traits have been the effects of maternal employment?

If it is impossible to extricate one particular aspect of social change from others with which it is intertwined, it is equally hard to isolate a mother's work outside the home from other factors which play their part in the close network of personal relations within the family. Each concrete situation is different, and in each the personalities of all concerned — husband, wife and children — as well as the general atmosphere (whether there is domestic harmony or disharmony), the economic position, and the social and educational background of the family play their part.

It seems, for instance, from some American and Swedish studies that the question of whether or not a working mother enjoys her work is as important an influence on the situation as whether she works at all. The nature of her job has almost as much bearing as the fact whether she is physically and mentally able to cope with the double burden of employment and family; but then, the nature of her job and her ability to cope are closely connected in a more than one-way casual relationship; and both may be connected with other factors, such as, e.g. her intelligence, her ability to organize, level of education, or her economic position.

There are also class differences in family patterns and in aspirations which further influence the situation.

The amount of time a mother is away from home — i.e. whether she works full-time or part-time — and the nature of substitute care are of very great importance, as is, of course, also the age of the children.

Another important factor is the role of the father, his attitude to his wife's employment — and hers to the fact that she contributes to providing for the family. Where both parents accept their status as joint breadwinners, a relation of partnership may exist which is wholly beneficial. Where the role of the father, on the other hand, is devalued because he is incapable of being the sole provider, the psychological effect, particularly on sons, may be damaging. This would be more likely to happen in a period of transition when — as still is the case in many suburban middle-class areas — the employment of married women is the exception rather than the rule and the role of the father as the only breadwinner is still undisputed.

This leads to the further point which has a bearing on the situation, namely, the approval or disapproval of neighbours and peers. In some working-class areas the employment of mothers has been traditional and widespread — e.g. in Lancashire — for a century or more. Life in these districts is geared to the fact of mothers going out to work. There is no evidence that the rate of juvenile delinquency or the incidence of other behaviour disorders among young people is higher than elsewhere.

The difficulties of isolating the factor "maternal employment" sufficiently to study its effects on the mental development of children has not, of course, deterred psychologists and social scientists from making the attempt. A whole number of investigations exist which are relevant to this topic.

The most widely known are John Bowlby's "Maternal Deprivation and Mental Health" and the studies of juvenile delinquency by Sheldon and Eleanor Glueck, notably "Working Mothers and Delinquency".

Bowlby's work was not specifically concerned with the problem of working mothers (although it has popularly very often been related to it) but with "maternal deprivation" in early childhood which, in the cases studied, was associated with the emotional shock of sudden separation, due to hospitalization, death or desertion. Neither he nor his disciples have provided evidence that the case of mothers going out to work daily, leaving their child in the care of a substitute — be it a grandmother, another relative, or a day nursery — and returning home regularly each evening — that is to say, keeping home and family intact — falls into the same category of deprivation and causes similar emotional disturbances as the cases of complete separation of mother and child he investigated.

As for the Gluecks, their painstaking statistical studies led them to the conclusion that juvenile delinquency is associated with lack of maternal supervision, poor discipline at home — both of which are independent of the fact whether a mother goes out to work or stays at home — and lack of family cohesion.

Both hypotheses have since been subjected to tests and found wanting. Investigations undertaken to discover whether Bowlby's concept of "partial deprivation" is applicable to children of working mothers have proved negative. The Gluecks' studies were all carried out among workingclass children and, although other investigators have confirmed their findings in respect of children from working-class homes, they do not appear equally to apply to children of middle-class families.

These and other investigations, carried out in the United States, have been published by F. Ivan Nye and Lois W. Hoffman in the Volume *The Employed Mother in America*. Their common method and purpose is to study, in carefully controlled tests, the effects of maternal employment on specific factors such as symptoms of anxiety, anti-social behaviour, school adjustment, intelligence scores, and various other personality characteristics. If the gist of some 25 separate studies may briefly be summed up in a sentence, it is that maternal employment as such appears to be of no importance as an influence on the lives of children. Personality characteristics of the mother, the nature of substitute care, social class, rural-urban differences, and such factors as whether or not a mother enjoys her work, are each statistically more significant than the simple dichotomy working — not-working.

At least two of the studies included in the volume suggest that "to the extent that a mother's working may have implications for her chldren" these "may be different for the two sexes", namely be more favorable for girls than boys — a fact which, as already indicated, appears to be connected with the devaluation of the father's role in the family.

Among the more unexpected findings is the one that employed mothers show a significantly better adjustment to their children than do mothers at home.

From these and other studies carried out elsewhere, one is led to the impression that most children — provided always that the necessary physical care and emotional stability are there (two important provisos) — adjust themselves without difficulty to the given conditions in which they find themselves.

Opinion polls among school children have shown that, by and large, those whose mothers were working were in favour of married women going out to work; those whose mothers were at home were against employment; while boys whose mothers had part-time jobs thought it was a good thing for married women to have an outside occupation part of the time — or else they might be bored at home — but they should not work all day as this would be too tiring for them. It would seem, therefore, that children on the whole — always allowing for individual differences of temperament — tend to be satisfied with the status quo, and there are always sensible rationalizations at hand to justify the position taken.

If this is the case, one may well wonder whether the employment pattern which is now establishing itself among married women might not lead to some emotional difficulties of its own. It is, as we have seen, becoming increasingly customary that married women give up their jobs when their children are born, stay at home during their infancy, and return to work when the children are in their teens. This pattern is, of course, dictated by practical necessity as well as by the wish of most mothers to look after their own young children. It is endorsed also by psychological doctrine which emphasizes the vital importance of a mother's full-time presence and devotion during the first years of a child's life.

Without in any way wishing to dispute the correctness of these assumptions, it may be worth considering that the resulting pattern also has its problems. The fact of mother starting off on a new life of relative independence at a time when her children are in their adolescence may, by the mere change of the accepted domestic routine, produce a shock effect, at least temporarily. It may, moreover, possibly aggravate a situation which, in itself, is full of emotional difficulties. On the other hand, it is, of course, also possible that the growing-up process may be helped on its way by the fact that mother's interests are no longer exclusively concentrated on her children. The dangers of possessiveness, the reluctance of mothers to relinquish their hold over their children, may be reduced and the independence for which adolescents crave — and which they need to grow into adults — may be promoted by the fact that mother now has another outlet for her energies. Some of the typical conflicts of adolescence may, possibly, in this way be alleviated if not entirely avoided.

This is another point on which there is no scientific evidence and which can only be mentioned as a personal observation. It will, no doubt, again depend on a large number of incidental factors how these problems are resolved, or whether they need arise at all.

In this, as in all other questions concerning the effects of maternal employment, the only hopeful approach to a better understanding — and hence to policies based on informed opinion — is the carrying out of a very large number of detailed studies, investigating one by one each aspect of the problem in painstaking analysis, testing every hypothesis carefully by the introduction of test variables, and eliminating successively all factors which prove irrelevant.

This task will require the patient research of many psychologists, social scientists and statisticians over a number of years. A beginning has been made in the United States. It would be good to know that elsewhere, too, the problem is receiving the urgent attention it deserves.

Women in Soviet Society*

The complexity of the interrelationship of the roles of women, as wife, mother, consumer, and producer, makes it difficult simply to summarize or to characterize Soviet policy toward women in the Russian economy as a whole or in any part of it. These varied roles so interact that Soviet policy in one area may have unintended repercussions on the way in which women perform in other areas. There is still little evidence that Soviet planners have managed to achieve a single, coherent, over-all policy with respect to the economic utilization of women but, rather, that they have several imperfectly coordinated and sometimes contradictory policies. . . .

To begin with, war, revolution, and political repression over the past five decades drastically altered the sex ratio in the Soviet Union in favor of women. . . . Irregularities in the Soviet population pyramid caused by war and other vicissitudes are so great that many decades will be required to moderate them. Although the male deficit is now confined to the older age groups, the manpower shortage continues for other reasons. Most important, the birth rate during and immediately after the war was unusually low. As a result, during the past half dozen years additions to the labor force have been small and the pressure to utilize women, which was so insistent in the decade following the war, has continued up to the present. Furthermore, the shrunken generation of war babies is now entering the childbearing age, and, therefore, the annual number of births is significantly reduced. In another generation, these small numbers will in turn keep additions to the labor force and to the population below the normal level. Thus, irregularities in the population pyramid will be perpetuated through several generations.

The present population policy of the government is aimed at maintaining or increasing the rate of growth in population, because a large and rapidly growing population is viewed as an asset rather than a

* Excerpts from Norton D. Dodge, *Women in the Soviet Economy*. Baltimore: The Johns Hopkins Press, 1966. Reprinted by permission.

liability. Certain programs, such as family allowances and medals for mothers of large families, are designed to increase the birth rate. The combined effect of legalized abortions and more effective contraception will be, of course, to reduce the birth rate at the same time other measures are being taken to increase it. Nevertheless, in spite of these contradictions in Soviet population policy, the intent of the government is to increase fertility. Thus far, however, the results are not impressive.

Demographic factors have played, and will continue to play, an important part in determining the role of women in the Soviet economy. The present high rate of participation of women in the Soviet labor force is not without precedent, however. In 1926, when the country was largely agricultural, almost every woman participated in economic activity outside the home for a part of the year. What is unique in the Soviet situation today is the very high rate of participation by women in the economy of a country so industrially advanced. At the present time, the Soviet participation rate of close to 70 per cent in the working ages is almost twice as high as the rate in the United States. This high rate has been maintained despite a major structural shift in the population away from rural areas, where the participation rate has always been very high, into urban areas where the participation rate initially was much lower. Since 1926, however, the participation rate of urban women age 16 to 59 has increased from 40 to 67 per cent. This increase has almost completely offset the decline in the average participation rate which would otherwise have occurred as the industrialization process proceeded.

The continuance of a high rate of female participation at all ages, even through the childbearing and child-rearing ages, is another distinctive Soviet characteristic. In the age group 20 to 39, which encompasses the most important child-bearing and child-rearing ages, approximately 80 per cent of the women are employed, a remarkably high rate for a country as advanced industrially as the Soviet Union. Women begin to withdraw from employment in the socialized sector of the economy as they approach the retirement age, but many older women continue to work on private agricultural plots.

In the Soviet Union economic pressures compelling women to work to make ends meet play a major role in keeping women in the labor force. The shortage of men has left many women without husbands, and they must work to support themselves and their families. Furthermore, for many families a single pay check provides only a bare subsistence, and many married women feel they must work in order to maintain an acceptable standard of living. Also, government and party action has altered social custom and public attitudes toward the employment of women. At the present time, few fields are considered inaccessible, and a woman is actually likely to feel defensive if she does not have a job. The regime has been particularly successful in opening the fields of science and technology to women. Attitudes toward women participating in these fields have so radically changed that they are freely accepted everywhere — except in work considered detrimental to their health.

The policies of the Soviet regime on the employment of women, protection on the job, and maternity benefits have been embodied in extensive legislation and executive orders issued since the Revolution. Often the legislation has not been enforced, particularly during the war emergency when women were in fact employed in many occupations from which by the existing law they were excluded for reasons of health. At the present time, however, the legal provisions concerning Soviet women are generally enforced, and in this respect the Soviet Union is among the more enlightened countries of the world.

Another factor affecting the participation of women in the labor force is the burden of family responsibilities. Although adequate data are lacking, the participation rate of Soviet women appears to decline, as is normally the case everywhere, as the number of their children increases. We have seen, however, that the Soviet participation rate holds up remarkably well, even in the face of this burden, throughout the child-bearing and child-rearing ages. This is possible partly because the varied child-care facilities provided in the Soviet Union free several millions of women with young children for employment outside the home. As has been pointed out, the demand for the services of these institutions continues to outrun the supply. According to estimates, approximately 12 per cent of the children of nursery age and 20 per cent of the children of kindergarten age can be accommodated in permanent child-care facilities. Substantially more can be accommodated in seasonal summer facilities. Most of the permanent facilities are concentrated in urban centers, and the seasonal facilities in the countryside. In a major city such as Moscow, almost half the children of nursery and kindergarten age are cared for in child-care centers, but in most communities there are long lists of children waiting to be admitted.

Although the government has allocated substantial investment funds over the years to the expansion of child-care facilities, it has been unwilling to assign to this program sufficient resources to satisfy demand. On the contrary, it has chosen to compel most working women to make their own arrangements — with members of the families or outside help — for the care of their young children. This policy can hardly be considered beneficial to the working mothers. From the standpoint of the regime's overriding goal of economic growth, however, the imposition of hardship on the working mother and a slightly lower rate of participation of women in the labor force have apparently been considered preferable to the diversion of investment funds and other resources to additional child-care facilities.

As the Soviet economy has passed through successive stages of development, there have, of course, been changes in the pattern of priorities. What was conceived as correct strategy during the period of forced industrialization under Stalin does not appear applicable today, at a higher stage of economic development when emphasis on producers' goods production is no longer so important. As a result, conditions in the Soviet Union are now favorable to greater investments in housing, production of consumers' goods, and child-care facilities with the aim of lightening the burden on women. Apparently the government expects to sustain or to increase the participation rate of women in this fashion rather than through the more Draconic policies pursued in the past.

Education was the first step by which Soviet women were enabled to equip themselves for a broader and more productive participation in the Soviet economy. Dramatic progress has been made in raising the educational levels of the population, and women have been, perhaps, the principal beneficiaries of this process. For all practical purposes, illiteracy among women has been wiped out except among the older generation and in some of the more stubbornly backward areas of the country. . . .

By concentrating its efforts on the younger age groups during the past four decades, the Soviet government has succeeded in raising substantially the level of educational attainment of millions of young men and women in those occupational fields critical for economic growth and development. Great numbers of younger women have been given on-the-job training in industry and have become an important element in the industrial labor force. Similarly, many young women have been afforded a specialized secondary or higher educational training in science and technology and in other key fields for economic development. Girls have been as well prepared as boys for admission to the scientific or technical faculties of specialized secondary and higher educational institutions because the curricula at the lower educational levels were made uniform for both sexes. Initially, minimum quotas were set for women to encourage their enrollment, and other efforts were made to increase female matriculation, especially in scientific and technical disciplines. As a result, women have had opened to them many of the more interesting and attractive occupations from which they had previously been excluded. This has been a major positive accomplishment of the Soviet regime.

The remarkable success of the Soviet Union in attracting women to the fields of science and technology is apparent from the statistics on education which we have surveyed. The great demand for women with scientific and technological training which arose in the 1930's initiated the impressive increase in the proportion of women enrolled in these fields. Although comprehensive statistics on the proportion of women enrolled in specific fields of science and technology are not available, such data as we do have show that women make up approximately three quarters of the enrollment in courses in the technology of food and consumers' goods production and approximately three fifths of those studying chemical engineering, hydrology, meteorology, geodesy, and cartography. In fields such as mining engineering, transportation, and machine building, on the other hand, only a fifth to a sixth of the students are women. But 53 per cent of the medical students and 25 per cent of the agricultural students are women, both percentages having dropped sharply in recent years. It is estimated that at Soviet universities three fourths to four fifths of the students enrolled in biology, more than two thirds of those in chemistry, two fifths to a half in mathematics, and a quarter to two fifths in physics, geology, and the agricultural sciences are women. In comparison with other countries of the world, these are strikingly high percentages.

There has been a major shift in the over-all proportion of women enrolled in specialized secondary and higher education since World War II. During and immediately after the war, the proportion of women enrolled reached its peak. In the past decade, however, the proportion of women has declined — slightly in specialized secondary education and sharply in higher education. This decline has occurred in every field, but is particularly pronounced in medicine, agriculture, and the socio-economic disciplines. The immediate causes limiting the proportion of women in higher education have been changes in the organization of the secondary school system and more especially in the regulations governing admission to higher educational institutions. Although equality of the sexes remains the stated policy of the Soviet regime, actual admission policies indicate an increasing departure from this principle. Although we cannot be certain that the reduction in the proportion of female enrollment has in fact stemmed from considerations of efficiency, such a reduction does admit of justification on economic grounds. In fields such as medicine, an excessively high proportion of women (from the standpoint of efficient utilization) was permitted to receive training. The government is now eager to restore a more desirable balance of the sexes. In other fields also, where the proportion of women was always lower, the proportion is being further reduced in the interest of efficiency, since the productivity of professional women in most fields tends to be less than that of men.

Even though education has prepared many Soviet women for professional careers, most Soviet women are still engaged in heavy, unskilled work. According to 1959 census data, four fifths of the total 56 million women employed in the labor force were engaged in what is officially termed "physical" labor, and of these the majority were employed in agricultural occupations. Nonspecialized agricultural work alone accounts for one third of the women engaged in physical labor. Typically, women are the field workers and livestock tenders, while men handle the skilled mechanical and construction work and serve as administrators. When the other more skilled agricultural occupations are included, agriculture accounts for 63 per cent of all women employed in physical labor. The large number of women still working in the fields, in spite of Soviet industrial advances, is one of the distinctive features of the Soviet economy.

Women have also come to play an important role in the nonagricultural sectors of the economy — particularly in industry and in the service sector. Throughout a wide range of occupations the percentage of women is substantially higher than that in the United States. Only in such traditional areas of female employment as secretarial, sales, and clerical work and nursing are the American percentages equally high. A high percentage of women is employed in communal and household services and in public dining, and women are relatively well represented in the garment trades and in various occupations in the textile and food industries. Large numbers of women may also be found in metalwork, construction, and transportation. Although most of the industrial and unskilled occupations have little intrinsic appeal for women, for those who lack training or talent for professional work they offer an opportunity to supplement the family income. Also, the high percentage of Soviet women in such occupations dramatically reflects the shortage of males of working age and the determination of the regime to maintain high rates of economic growth at the cost, if necessary, of individual welfare.

Perhaps even more distinctive than the high over-all participation rate of Soviet women, and the vital role they play in the older age groups of the labor force, is their heavy representation in white-collar occupations and the professions. This is the bright side of the employment picture for Soviet women. The role of women in white-collar occupations has increased greatly since the Revolution and has assumed proportions unequaled elsewhere in the world. Today, women comprise more than half the labor force employed in "mental" work. . . . Thus, women form a clear majority of the semiprofessional and professional labor force in the Soviet Union. The woman physician, engineer, research worker, or technician is a commonplace. American women, in contrast, make up very small minorities in most professions, the only exception being teaching; and in such fields as engineering, physics, and medicine, the professional woman is a rarity. For example, while women comprise only 7 per cent of the physicians in the United States, they make up 75 per cent of the total in the Soviet Union. In engineering, the contrast is even more striking; over a quarter of a million Soviet women are engineers, and make up a third of the profession, while in the United States, female engineers account for less than 1 per cent of the total. The number of women in the natural sciences in the Soviet Union is also substantial, although the proportion of women varies considerably from field to field, tending to be higher in the biological sciences and chemistry and lower in a field such as physics.

In 1947, the only year for which data are available, women made up 35 per cent of the staffs of Soviet higher educational institutions, while in the United States they constituted 22 per cent in 1954–55. In the Soviet Union, 68 per cent of the philologists were women, 48 per cent of the teachers of medicine and biology, 45 per cent of the chemists, and 40 per cent of the education teachers. In the remaining fields, the proportion of women lay below the average of 36 per cent for all fields combined. . . . Only in education, and to a lesser degree in the arts, are the percentages of women at all comparable in the two countries. In all other corresponding fields, the Soviet percentages are substantially higher, evincing the success of the Soviets in utilizing the talents of women in fields which in the United States and other western countries remain almost exclusively male domains.

Although the prospects for a woman's embarking upon a professional career in the Soviet Union are much more favorable than in the United States or other Western countries, the prospects for her professional advancement are not so happy; for the proportion of Soviet women in the higher professional echelons tends to decrease as the rank advances. This phenomenon can be observed even in fields, such as education and health where women predominate. . . . In medicine and health, although women make up 75 per cent of the medical profession, they account for only 57 per cent of the directors, deputy directors, and chief physicians of medical establishments. In research institutions where women make up half the scientific workers (mauchnye rabotniki), they account for about a third of heads and deputy heads of branches, 21 per cent of the division heads and their deputies, and 16 per cent of the directors and their deputies and other top administrative personnel. This pattern of declining representation of women as rank increases is repeated in all fields for which data are available.

The lodging of a disproportionate share of women in the lower and intermediate professional levels suggests that the Soviet government is not receiving so high a return on its educational investment in women as in men, since Soviet professional women with comparable educational training show, on the whole, a lower level of achievement than men. Further evidence of this is provided by various indexes of scholarly productivity. For example, among the top Soviet scientists — full and corresponding members of the Academies of Sciences — very few women are to be found. Women also make up a very small proportion of the recipients of Lenin prizes. An extensive survey of scholarly publications gives further unmistakable evidence that the scholarly productivity of women is lower than that of men. In a comparison of the proportion of women in various specialties on the staffs of higher educational institutions with the proportion of scholarly articles contributed in each field by women, it was found that on the average women contributed about half as many articles as would be expected from their numbers.

The Soviets have done little or no research on the possible effects of various social or environmental factors on the achievement of women. To what extent their lower productivity and their smaller proportions at the higher administrative and professional levels may be due to innate rather than to socially or culturally determined factors is a question that cannot be easily answered. Unlike the woman farmer or factory worker doing a routine job, the Soviet professional woman is likely to derive considerable satisfaction from her work and to be seriously interested in it. But even though her motivation is high, the obstacles to achievement are considerable. Some of the important factors inhibiting a woman's productivity are lost work time and distractions due to family responsibilities, the interruption of a career because of child-bearing, and job assignment difficulties. Such factors cannot, of course, readily be eradicated. Other conditions which involve the intellectual development of girls and their career motivations can perhaps be improved. Great progress has already been made in altering the image of a woman's role in society. The intellectual, career-oriented girl in the Soviet Union today can find much support and social approval compared with the girl of only a few decades ago. It appears, however, that conflicts between career and marriage and motherhood will remain for some time to come, since the greater involvement of a woman with her family is not susceptible of drastic change even in Soviet society. If the regime should choose to divert a greater proportion of its investment funds toward the provision of child-care facilities and consumers' goods to lighten the burden of housework, women would be thereby relieved of some of the drain on their creative energies caused by family responsibilities, and their productivity should increase accordingly.

It is evident from this survey that the Soviet regime has a very different attitude toward women from that of a largely unplanned, individualistic society such as our own. Reflecting a philosophy which conceives of the individual's welfare as the basic social goal, our society views the education of women, as well as that of men, to be desirable as an end in itself. Although much of our education is career-oriented, the failure of a young woman after her marriage to pursue a career for which she has been trained does not mean that her education is considered wasted. The raising of a family is considered in itself a sufficient contribution to the welfare of society and is not normally viewed as a distraction from which a woman should, is possible, be relieved so that she can pursue a "productive" career. In contrast, the Soviets see women as an economic asset or resource, to be developed and exploited as effectively as possible. This attitude reflects, of course, the regime's overriding goal of promoting economic development, a goal which has governed Soviet economic policies since the late 1920's. Concurrently, the regime has been concerned with the enlargement of women's rights and with freeing women from all forms of repression and discrimination. This idealistic motif in Soviet policy cannot be denied, but it must be viewed in the proper perspective.

As we have seen, Soviet policy toward women is complex and sometimes contradictory. However, if the predominance of the economic motive in determining Soviet policies toward women is recognized and borne in mind, many of the apparent contradictions can be better understood. It is true that, on occasion, policies inspired by idealism have coincided with those motivated by strictly material considerations, but wherever they diverge, the Soviets have consistently chosen to pursue the economic rather than the idealistic goal. In the first years following the Revolution, for example, the regime was altruistically concerned with securing women's rights and bringing about a greater equality of the sexes. A great deal of legislation was passed to these ends, and the percentage of women in specialized secondary and higher educational institutions, as well as the percentage employed in industry and other branches of the economy, increased significantly during the 1920's and 1930's. But women were perhaps too successful in securing "equality." Too much equality can become a burden to women whose physiological function of motherhood makes impossible their avoidance of heavy responsibilities over and above those imposed by their work. Soviet time-use studies show clearly that the total burden of employment in the labor force and in the home falls much more heavily upon women than upon men. Although Soviet legislation recognizes that physiological differences necessitate certain safeguards to a woman's health and welfare, the laxity of enforcement and even the suspension of some of these safeguards during various periods of

Soviet history suggest that the goal of greater production has more often than not overridden the altruistic concern for protection. Naturally, even under the most extreme pressures, the regime cannot afford a complete abandonment of safeguards and protective measures, since the effective utilization of women as producers depends to a considerable degree upon the reduction of the conflicts which arise from the woman's competing roles as wife and mother. But if the regime had consistently placed women's welfare ahead of production in its scale of priorities, there would be concrete evidence of this in a greater abundance of child-care facilities and a more conscientious enforcement of protective legislation. Similarly, if equality of educational opportunity between the sexes had been of primary concern, admissions regulations and other factors which have contributed to the decline over the past decade in the proportion of women among students in higher education would have been altered when the decline first became evident. Failure to alter them until recently is evidence that the regime in fact preferred the efficient use of its limited higher educational facilities to the social ideal of equality. Apparently realizing that a woman is not likely to be so economically productive as a man in the course of a lifetime, Soviet planners opted for productivity as a social goal and chose accordingly to restrict access to higher education to a smaller proportion of women. It remains to be seen whether the recent modifications in admission requirements are sufficient to redress the balance between the sexes and to permit the percentage of women in higher education to rise to a level proportionate with the percentage of women in the college age population as a whole.

In a totalitarian society such as the Soviet Union, many options are open to the regime in pursuing its policies which are not available to a government responsive to the public will. The party, both directly and through the government, exercises a decisive influence on almost every aspect of economic and social behavior. As we have seen, certain of the policies adopted may be mutually counter-productive — as are, for instance, those aimed simultaneously at the achievement of a higher birth rate and a greater participation of women in the labor force. Others may be in conflict with deep-seated beliefs and customs and may make slow headway — as, for example, the higher education of women in Central Asia, where the traditional subservence of women leads to the early withdrawal of girls from school. For the most part, however, through its control of the means of mass communication and education, the regime has succeeded in achieving acceptance of the new attitudes toward female participation in the labor force, particularly in sectors and occupations which had previously been all but closed to women.

To a society such as our own, which does not tap more than a fraction of the full economic potential of its women, both a lesson and a challenge are implied in the success of the Soviets in developing skilled and capable professional women, particularly in the fields of science and technology. Indeed, Soviet numerical superiority in certain scientific and technological fields is due entirely to the employment of a large number of women in these fields. Although it has been pointed out that the achievement of Soviet women, on the average, falls short of that of men, there can be no doubt that many talents and skills which would have been neglected in another society have been developed and utilized in the Soviet Union and that Soviet policies have made of women one of the major sources of economic strength. Indeed, the imbalance of the sexes in the Soviet population, particularly in the mature age groups, has made the effective participation of women in all sectors of the economy essential to its development. In other, more advanced, societies, this urgent need for the services of women does not arise. The Soviet example proves, however, that a large reservoir of female talent in the United States and other Western countries remains untapped or underdeveloped. Although the tools and mechanisms required to exploit this potential may not be so readily available to our governments, nor the motivation to exploit it so pressing, it is clear that our own society could go much farther than it presently does toward a full utilization of its womanpower. Indeed, the question might be raised whether we can really afford — not only from the standpoint of the national interest, but also from that of the welfare of women as individuals — to neglect their potential contribution of talent and intellect and to leave them so largely at the margin of our economic life.

The Swedes Do it Better*

Some rational answers to questions that trouble many American women today — and perhaps some illuminating guidelines for the future — can be found in the experience of Sweden. Our countries, to be sure, are different in many respects: Sweden is a small nation with a homogeneous population. But both nations are attached to a democratic political philosophy, and Sweden comes closer to matching our high standard of living than any other European country. While there are many resemblances between our two societies, the Swedes have come closer to resolving issues which are still being uneasily debated in the United States.

Why, for instance, is the familiar conflict between work and marriage so much less of a problem in Sweden? One reason — though by no means the only one — is the fact that Swedish women devote less time and energy to child bearing.

Sweden has, in fact, one of the lowest birth rates in the world, fourteen per thousand population in 1960 compared with twenty-four per thousand in the United States. This is not due to any great difference in ability to control family size. A substantial majority of non-Catholic Americans and Swedes are effective contraceptors. Nor are economic factors the heart of the matter. In fact the relative cost of rearing a child is greater in America than in Sweden, where an expanding system of welfare legislation has provided increasing financial benefits to mothers and children. This aid began in the 1930s to spur the low birth rate which was below replacement level for several years.

All Swedish mothers, married or not, now receive a grant of $180 when a child is born, as well as free delivery and confinement, grants for postnatal health care for mother and child, and an allowance of $180 a year for each child up to the age of sixteen. (Unmarried mothers

* Richard F. Tomasson, "The Swedes Do It Better." Copyright © 1962 by Harper's Magazine Inc. Reprinted from the October, 1962 issue of *Harper's Magazine* by permission of the author. Minor revisions in the original have been made by Professor Tomasson.

receive additional cash compensation in recognition of their greater need when a father does not contribute to the support of a child.) Comprehensive national health insurance makes the child's medical bills negligible and complete dental care is available to all children in the schools. Nor need Swedish parents worry about paying for their children's education. Through the university level, tuition is virtually free and there are generous scholarship and loan programs to help meet students' living costs.

Employers are forbidden by law to discharge a woman employee who gets married or becomes pregnant. She is entitled to a substantial proportion of her pay for a maternity leave of up to six months. With all these inducements one would expect Swedish fertility to exceed ours.

There are, however, important differences in Swedish and American culture which explain the significant disparity in family size. (The Swedish population will probably increase by only 10 per cent between 1960 and 1975 while ours will take a 25 or 30 per cent leap.)

Of prime importance is the simple fact that Swedes marry about four years later than Americans — the median age for Swedish men in the 1950s was twenty-seven; for women, twenty-four. Americans, in fact, marry earlier than the people of any other industrialized nation. This is, of course, one reason for our population explosion. Very young couples have a longer period of fecundity, more energy to deal with the rigors of child-rearing, and a less realistic picture of the burdens of parenthood than those who marry later. It is also true that a girl who goes to marriage directly from her parents' home or the college dormitory adjusts more easily to the confining role of motherhood than one who has had several years of bachelor freedom. And early marriage tends to narrow a woman's horizon to the traditional roles of wife and mother before competing interests have a chance to develop.

Most American wives have worked outside their homes before marriage, a majority do so again some time after marriage, but few — even among college graduates — can be said to have careers. In Sweden, on the other hand, a high proportion of middle-class wives have relatively uninterrupted working lives and there are far more women in the traditionally male occupations than in America.

In Swedish universities, for example, women are now a quarter of the students of medicine, dentistry, and the natural sciences, and 15 per cent of those in law school; a majority of the pharmacy students are women. In all these fields in the United States the proportion of women is small or negligible. Few Swedish wives give up careers when they marry; few American wives have careers to give up.

A Shack in the Country

Family size and behavior are affected too by a difference in attitudes toward city living. Smaller quarters and the distractions and opportunities of the city discourage large families. In all industrial societies urban families have fewer children than those who live in the country. Statistically, Americans are as urbanized as the Swedes but — as William F. Whyte and Jane Jacobs have eloquently charged — we are essentially anti-city; if we can afford it we prefer to live in the suburbs despite the difficulties and deprivations that go with commuting.

The Swedes, on the other hand, do not share our feeling that we are not doing right by our children if we bring them up in the city. Families are generally content to live in apartments in Stockholm or Gothenburg, though many wish they were larger and easier to get. A vacation shack in the country satisfies their bucolic longings.

An even more striking difference is in the permissive single standard of sexual behavior which prevails in Sweden. There are social pressures against promiscuity, but on the whole unmarried young women have about the same latitude as young men. Thus there is little of the guilt and moral ambiguity about sex relations among the unmarried which act as such a powerful inducement to early marriage in the United States.

Interestingly, Sweden has a divorce rate lower by a third than ours. Considering how far Sweden has moved along the road to full equality for women, it is perhaps paradoxical that the roles of husband and wife are more specifically defined than in the United States. This is, in fact, generally true of Europeans who feel that American husbands do much "woman's work." Swedish (or Dutch, French, or Austrian) fathers will seldom be found diapering, feeding, or bathing their children; nor are they dish driers, grocery shoppers, or baby-sitters. But this is changing among younger Swedes. Only in America is it not surprising for a university professor to feel that he must be home by five o'clock in order to help his wife with the children. And it may be that the amiable co-operation of their husbands in some of the onerous duties of child care is an extra inducement to American mothers to have more babies.

More probably, however, the decision to have a third or fourth child results from the mother's feeling that she is on full-time duty at home anyhow and has no compelling outside involvements. It takes an exceptionally well organized woman with great vitality to flout convention and play the mother and career roles simultaneously against all the obstacles American middle-class culture puts in her way. Certainly the conventional wisdom makes it clear that home is the only place for the mother of small — and even not so small — children. Family, neighbors, and friends urge her to stay there as do such diverse instructors as Dr. Spock, Ann Landers, and Russell Kirk. Even the government conspires by allowing only slight tax exemption for the child-care expenses of working mothers.

Swedish women too are under some pressure to stay home with their babies, and most of them take more than just a few months out to have them. But a relatively high proportion of middle-class wives with small children work outside their homes. Facilities for the daytime care of small children are more readily available than in the United States and so are competent domestic helpers. But the crucial difference is the fact that it is not generally considered strange, antisocial, or immoral for the Swedish mother of young children to work outside her home.

Recent evidence accumulated in the United States suggests that we too may have reason to reverse our stand on these questions. For example, the sociological journal, *Marriage and Family Living*, devoted its November 1961 issue to the subject, "Women and Work." Three diverse studies that it reviewed (by Lee G. Burchinal and Jack E. Rossman, Evan T. Peterson, and Joseph B. Perry, Jr.) all came to the conclusion that maternal employment per se does not have the adverse effects on children's lives attributed to it. One study which covered more than a thousand children in the public schools of Cedar Rapids, Iowa indicated that the academic performance and social adjustment of children — from nursery school through high school — had no perceptible connection with their mothers' employment. Similarly, a study of some six hundred Michigan high-school girls demonstrated that while an employed mother may be under increased physical strain, her dual role does not affect the mother-daughter relationship adversely. The same conclusions were corroborated by interviews conducted in Spokane with 104 nonemployed mothers, 104 who were employed, and 82 mother substitutes. Nothing was found to support the widely held hypothesis that the separation of children from their mothers "has 'bad' psychological, physical, and social effects on children. . . ."

AMERICA'S FERTILITY CHAMPS

Findings of this sort have not yet gained much currency. But as the facts become more widely known, they are bound to contribute to a more rational and less child-centered way of life for American women. There are indeed already signs that our birth rate is declining and that families will be smaller in the years ahead. I have asked hundreds of college students over the past couple of years how many children they wanted. As might be expected they overwhelmingly want two, three, or four. But the interesting fact is that more want two than four. Compared to the 1940s and 1950s, this is a significant change. The uninterrupted decline in the American birth rate between 1957 and 1963 from 25.3 to 21.6 births per 1,000 population may well reflect a real decline in average family size.

It may well be, in fact, that American women born in the early 'thirties will turn out to be the fertility champions of the twentieth century. On the other hand, wives of the 1970s and 1980s may find themselves as free as Swedish women are today from the conflict between the traditional woman's role and the opportunities which an affluent industrial society provides.

The distance still to be bridged is epitomized in two sociological studies. Writing about "Student Culture at Vassar," John H. Bushnell observed in Nevitt Sanford's recent Anthology, *The American College:*

"The Vassar student's future identity is largely encompassed by the projected role of wife-mother. . . . For these young women the 'togetherness' vogue is definitely an integral theme of future family life with any opportunities for independent action attaching to an Ivy League degree being willfully passed over in favor of the anticipated rewards of close-knit companionship within the home that-is-to-be."

In sharp contrast, Kaare Svalastoga, a Danish sociologist, in an article on "The Family in Scandinavia" notes:

"But even if she excels in all these respects [being a good housekeeper and hostess, a loving mother, and an attractive spouse], she will reap slight social esteem, because dominant middle-class opinion will insist on the superior value of choosing a career outside the home and of cultivating literary and artistic interests."